APPLIED VISUALIZATION

APPLIED VISUALIZATION

A Mind-Body Program

James Lynn Page

1991
Llewellyn Publications
St. Paul, Minnesota 55164-0383, U.S.A.

quantum © W. Foulsham & Co. Ltd.

First U.S. Edition, 1991
First Printing, 1991

Cover art by Tom Canny

Library of Congress Cataloging-in-Publication Data
  Page, James Lynn.
    Applied visualization: a mind-body program / James Lynn Page.
  —1st Llewellyn ed., rev.
      p.   cm.
    Includes bibliographical references and index.
    ISBN 0-87542-597-6
    1. Visualization. 2. Self-realization. 3. Success—Psychological
  aspects. 4. Mind and body. I. Title.
  BF367.P34   1991   90-27419
  153.3′ 2—dc20   CIP

This Llewellyn/Quantum edition produced for
U.S.A. and Canada under license by:

Llewellyn Publications
A Division of Llewellyn Worldwide, Ltd.
P.O. Box 64383, St. Paul, MN 55164-0383, U.S.A.

If one advances confidently in the direction of his dreams and endeavours to live the life which he has imagined, he will meet with a success unexpected in the common hour.

Henry David Thoreau

CONTENTS

INTRODUCTION

My intention in writing this book is to explore more fully the ramification of the age-old technique of visualisation, namely that matter is unequivocably affected by mind. I sound out in no uncertain terms what has been promulgated by the likes of Emerson, Jung, Allen, Eddington, Flammarion, etc., not to mention the plethora of d.i.y. manuals on the psyche published this century. It is upon this axiom that the book is based, and the spaces are filled exploring its many implications and how they apply to the individual both in the external world and that mysterious invisible world within, for in the final analysis there is no real distinction between the two. The case histories presented here exemplify this truth and how it may be discovered by a search for one's soul. Yet the majority of them concern the nature of personal tragedy for it is a rare individual who seeks out the inner motives for his or her actions when everything is going well. There is no greater goad for looking inward than suffering the pains of having 'failed' at life, and one must in the end own up to individual, or at least shared, responsibility. Of course, the mind related to matter axiom can also be exemplified in happier instances where periods of creativity and fulfilment can be traced back to a change of attitude or the conscious exercising of the magical properties of 'mind-power', and indeed the almost fairy-tale-like account of Louise (in Chapter 4) makes sure that no-one could possibly fail to miss the point.

Despite visualisation being firmly rooted in occult tradition, the archetypal twentieth-century civilised human being prefers to avoid subjects which suggest (to them) encounters with nature spirits, angels and demons, pagan deities or the wizened old figure complete with traditional straggly beard and conical hat. Instead he or she opts for the far more rational approach of behavioural psychology, the philosophies of Bertrand Russell, the concepts of Freud, or takes the IQ test in attempts at self-knowledge because psychic matters contain too many grey areas. But ceremonial magic stripped of its more decorative and sometimes pretentious accompaniments is nothing more than, to paraphrase Crowley, the art of causing changes in conformity with the will, and if willing something to happen is an indirect cause of such changes then visualisation is magic *per se*. However, visualisation is such a straightforward discipline that it need not be explained via occult terminology or any circuitous routes whatever for there is basically nothing new to learn. Moreover, it has found its way into the modern psychologies of thoroughly normal, non-occult writers with professional qualifications and a standing as the embodiment of respectability — not the kind of people the layman would associate with those 'weirdos' (please note inverted commas) who wear talismans and browse around psychic fairs looking for crystals and incense burners. That visualisation is an occult practice is undisputable, yet writers of inspirational material are often at pains to coat it with a veneer of respectability (à la Dr Peale, see Bibliography) under the heading of self-help psychology in order to avoid the word 'magic'. But whether ancient wisdom reappears under another name, is incorporated into 'how to live' manuals, or is glimpsed under the evening skies with an enquiring heart, it remains wisdom nonetheless, and visualisation is one of its begetters.

And this is not, dare I say, your average book on the subject of visualisation, for the majority of works I have encountered on imagery presuppose that the reader is in a position to be able to use it. By that I mean generally healthy in a psychological sense, and thus it transpires that the already mentally healthy individual is the one assumed to have greater access to the powers of the inner mind. I have yet to read a penetrating work on visualisation containing guidance for those in the midst of personal suffering, loneliness, terminal boredom, anxiety, frustration and related symptoms of private purgatory, for these states are not wholly mental in effect; they are most often residues of acquired emotional patterns. If emotion is the source of power upon which the inner mind is contingent for successful visualisation, then these eroding energy-consuming emotional habits can themselves be dissolved by the same authority that first put them there. And an authority they are, for who is the individual who has not felt this subtle invasion of the undesirable despite good intentions to think happy thoughts?

Some of the first chapter is aimed at individuals who may be suffering inwardly because 'something' has gone, or is going wrong with their lives and feel powerless to do anything about it. Needless to say, the abiding sense of futility and apathy only serves to prolong the syndrome since the mind is apt to concentrate on its loss, drawing itself into a painful vicious circle until 'even that which they have shall be taken away'. Yet the individual determined to relieve personal suffering is still found at the mercy of his or her emotions, no matter how much the super-rational ego tries to make the pain go away. This split between thought and feeling needs to be healed, and the positive thinking of writers like the popular Dr Peale will amount to little if the bridge between the ego and the unconscious is in serious need of repair. One of the tools available in this situation is visualisation.

Thus, in the following pages are the results of an enquiry into the nature of the mind, that demonstrate that the powers invested in thought which lead to personal tragedy, spring from the same source as the ones that bring happiness and fulfilment. Do we always have to suffer in order to become wise after the event? My answer to that question is twofold: 'yes', we need to become more aware, or wise, but it need not ultimately occur through pain, though it is typical of human nature that we must learn the hard way. However, this does not mean that coming to wisdom through pain is intrinsic to the nature of the individual; it is merely a consequence of a general lack of self-knowledge and knowledge about the universe. I intend to show that trial and error is unnecessary and that with more knowledge of the psyche in its relation to nature, the power lies within to create the future desired, utilising the faculties of imagination and feeling. And it comes as no surprise that these two powers are the ones one would exercise the least in bringing about that bright future, as they have been relegated to the boroughs of fantasy and sentiment owing to the Westerner's insistence on the virtues of logic and attachment to the material world. But as we shall see, sometimes despite themselves, imagination and emotion are often the real power behind the throne.

The ability to give birth to a new way of life through inner images still seems nothing short of a miracle and I must confess to having had severe doubts when I first encountered the subject. My incredulity was sparked off when I came across Al Koran's *Bring Out the Magic In Your Mind* because the direct approach and simplicity was felt too good to be true; it was as if I wanted visualisation to be difficult and contain weird paradoxes in order to satisfy the enquiring conscious mind. When I first read Koran's book I was struck with a suspicion that prevented me from taking much of it seriously — in short, I thought it was the work of a madman. How could something so foolishly simple not be? But its value rests in its own simplicity and I have since come to love every word of it.

The reason that there will always exist those who reject the idea of thought power, is because it cannot be proven to work as one might demonstrate the boiling point of water in a chemistry lab. The workings of the mind cannot be set up as the object of a physical experiment whose results are filed away neatly into little boxes, for mind can neither be seen with the eyes nor held in one's hands. There is the individual who will stubbornly proclaim , 'If I can't see it, then it doesn't exist', and this is precisely the kind of remark one will hear whenever the issue of the inner worlds is raised. Yet there is also a sizeable number of perceptive human beings who can see what refuses to appear to the eyes: they can see the unbreakable link between the general patterning of their thoughts and the external conditions surrounding them, for one is a reflection of the other.

It was some years after first reading Koran's book when I realised that simple truths need not be expressed in long, erudite works that delve into every recess of the inner mind, where the opinions of the author are canvassed scientifically and soberly, although for the same reason, less effectively. Many of these works lacked the quality I had found so attractive in Koran — the ability to inspire the reader with enthusiasm. That, and a kind of childlike faith which spares the need to discover precisely how the internal mechanism of visualisation operates, for enthusiasm and the incentive to act are the obligatory complements to visualisation, that point to nothing other than self-fulfilling achievement. In turn, one attracts further successes, a phenomenon echoed in Emerson's aphorism that 'much will have more'.

Thus, a certain kind of mentality or attitude is required in the approach to visualisation. This attitude is comprised of an openness to life, faith in the future and the eagerness to weave new possibilities into the fabric of the present, not to mention at least some acknowledgment of the mind's ability to create. And it requires naivety, but in this sense I do not mean the kind of naivety one shows on the first day at work when asked to go and fetch a bucket of steam, and not blindness about other people. This brand of naivety is the product of a mind stripped of cast-iron preconceptions about the way life is; it is a mind prepared to believe in its dream and remain unmoved by the comments of the cynical; it is an attitude encouraging faith in one's makeshift reality until it is realised as matter of fact. Moreover, this naivety does not lift one on to cloud nine draped in illusions about reality, quite the contrary, for it opens up to the flow of life and the energies manifesting both within and without the individual, as the lopsided and soulless views of life begin gently to disappear.

CHAPTER 1
THE ART OF LIVING

Those who have fed at the breast of Mother Nature, quite reasonably, would never bite the hand that feeds it. There are those, however, who go in complete ignorance of the great lady — and do they starve.

Turbulence is life force. It is an opportunity. Let's love turbulence and use it for a change.
Ramsay Clark

The late John Lennon, in an interview with a Fleet Street writer, once remarked upon the comments of a witch who was asked on television whether she was 'black' or 'white'. Her reply was to the effect that no such distinction exists and she referred to a power which can be used for either good or evil, although the intrinsic natures of these two polar opposites will forever remain a purely subjective matter. This power to create emanates from us whether or not we are aware of it, even without our conscious summoning of it by invocation, either in honour of the Sun God Osiris with the sacred Egyptian Flame Ritual, amidst the sweet smell of incense; or celebrating the black mass addressing Lucifer, uttering strange dialogues surrounded by all manner of foul substances. The source remains the same and works either to create or destroy the multifaceted situations which we encounter in our lives. Even though we ourselves are both the engineers of, and vehicles for this source, many of us continue to remain blissfully unconscious of ourselves.

Wrapping oneself in the illusions of the ego is one thing, but it becomes somewhat less than lovely when from out of the blue one is confronted with misfortune, which we are so blind as to call bad luck, so unexpected as to warrant the question, 'What the hell is happening to me?' or in some cases, 'O Lord, why hast thou forsaken me?'

These are the same often well-meaning people who continue to remain utterly unaware of the part they play in crushing an area of their lives that, with a change of attitude might have been a thriving, on-going success. And when one notices in the local book shop, literature with the title *When bad things happen to good people,* it is glaringly obvious that we are getting something wrong, somewhere along the line. If the authors of such seminal pieces of work and public champions of moral rectitude were to glimpse just a little of the nature of the psyche, then perhaps we would incur less condemnation and good people would not seem quite so good anymore, as the shades of grey reveal themselves from behind a starched white *persona.* The art of living is success in the broadest sense, being able to encompass and even live out the apparent conflict of opposites in nature; from kind to cruel, loved to unloved, innocent to guilty, even good to bad, and real success is seen in the person who can master this art, accept life in all of its multifarious aspects and still remain sane.

Those of us who have the perspicacity to acknowledge this inner source of creation will make a better job of their lives than the ones who cannot, and I am sure that you will have repeatedly come across the following aphorisms in your favourite self-help manuals: that the unconscious is a creative tool (which it is); that visualising for something will make it appear in your life (which it will); that to increase the power of your visualisation, you should act as if you had already been granted your wish (which you should). This creative force pervades every minute of every day in one's existence, either working hand in hand with one's will, or conversely making life hell for us, and I put it to you that the ultimate engineer of one's existence (especially in relation to fated events) is thought. If you are able to digest this fact, then you are ready to embark upon the journey marked out between the covers of this book, for it is a tenet on which rests the art of creating through the power of mental images.

Thus, successful living depends on an awareness of what, psychologically speaking, we are doing to ourselves; how we make the bed on which we must lie. Even the person of genuine insight who has realised that thought creates, is apt to forget this during the course of daily life and over-identify with the material world, temporarily forgetting that they are experiencing an effect of which they are partly the cause. Typically, we see the situation going on around us as something completely external, like an observer with their nose pressed up against a window. In a real sense, scenes that are played out in one's environment, whether they concern us directly or indirectly, bear a definite relationship to the psyche of the observer: the individual has attracted the situation, or is it the other way round? Only in seeing this can the mortal bring about a desirable transformation in the objective world that appears to be quite removed from personal influence, yet continues to rear its undesirable head when least expected. If caught in the web of resisting unwanted circumstances from which there is hardly any escape, the individual becomes a plaything of fate, since the more that negative reactions are sparked off, the longer will it take for the situation to heal. But once this is understood, the individual can bring about a revolution in his or her thinking, and this need not be a slow process, for at least complaints about things as they are will cease.

Life is full of the unexpected and one cannot resist the feeling that fortune has smiled whenever a chance event can be construed as good luck. It is tempting to interpret the event as a gift from the gods handed down on a silver platter never once suspecting that somewhere along the line one has played an unconscious part in constructing such a fate. But it is equally fascinating to come to terms with the fact that one's mind is one's fate, for wherever choice goes, destiny follows. What are not quite so readily savoured are those unexpected occurrences that show the reverse face of the coin of providence, that nevertheless were conceived within the mind and subsequently brought forth as a physical event. Blindness to the inner self will cause it to work behind our backs, choreographing the destruction, or at least stagnation, of aspects of our lives usually without the consent of the conscious mind and it is only later when unconscious energies come into play that the seal is set and it 'all seemed so sudden'. The suddenness is felt in the individual when his wife walks out on him; he finds himself spurned and rejected by the boss at work for no apparent reason; appointments and dates with friends are cancelled without explanation provoking the feeling that his world is slowly but surely falling to pieces.

WHEN IMAGES CAN BE DANGEROUS

It takes some insight and not just a little humbling to realise that it is oneself (or at least one's cooperation with another) who has given birth to the personal tragedy that twists and torments one into a state approaching that of a nervous wreck. My intention here is not to relay the usual panacea of positive-thinking techniques, but to deal with matters from the inside, the core of the issue when the mortal is confronted with an inner purgatory that is the consequence of most of twentieth-century man's mistakes. To take a typical example, which seems to have grown into epidemic proportions within the last forty years, let us consider the psychological effects of the suffering incurred through the break up of a love relationship. The Buddhist philosophy of non-attachment is reduced to idealism in the face of such emotional breakdowns, for human attributes like attachment, possessiveness and jealousy are ingrained into Western consciousness and cannot be made magically to disappear by shaving one's head and meditating in a bath of cold water. To be attached, we are told, is to inflict suffering upon ourselves, but the individual who needs to relate emotionally to others and thus become 'close' is violating nature if he or she walks the tightrope towards complete non-attachment. Sure enough, the psyche urges one to self-fulfilment, to express fully what we are, and part of what we are encompasses the need to reach others and fulfil certain emotional needs that are not satisfied by poring over Eastern texts on Swami Whatsisname or chanting Hare Krishna. The gulf between Eastern and Western consciousness is too wide for us to incorporate successfully Buddha into the daily grind of get up for work, eight hours at the factory, a pint in the pub and get to bed early enough to rise the next morning. The Western world does not consist of spiritually evolved beings reciting prayers every morning, it consists of what we call normal living, and this includes the attachment to others that is painful when we have to let go of someone and sever the invisible cord that binds. When the tears begin to flow and the curses at one's loss ring out, how might the average individual cope with the situation?

One only has to read the agony columns in the daily tabloids to see how commonplace losing someone is. Typically there is the sense of emptiness, unexpressed (or indeed, expressed) rage, lachrymose misery and in some cases volcanic emotions that burst forth to create a miasma of complicated feeling states, *ad nauseam*. The lingering depression so often a result of this rupture of the psyche is like an invasion of so many hostile aliens as the individual cries out in pain, 'Please God, make it go away', though God, the vicar, the psychiatrist or the artificial stimulant have not the power to make it 'go away', only oneself has.

On the inner level, one is confronted with remembered past actions and here is where images can truly be dangerous, for strong memories in the aftermath of such a tragedy play upon the mind, taunting, tantalising, increasing the sense of loss. On the outer level, the individual is accustomed to hearing advice such as 'do something to take your mind off it', and may participate in a host of activities that finally reveal themselves as nothing more than temporary ameliorations. It is the emotions which need attention, and our grieving subject will almost certainly make a poor job of dealing with them, fearing that the chasm may never be filled again.

Heavy times indeed, and it is a prickly area to delve into when dealing with the archetypal shipwreck case, for there is little that one can offer to ease the pain; the remedy, of which the individual will be intensely aware, must be prescribed from within. The individual may make one of the two classic moves in an attempt to keep painful memories at bay; they may elect to overcompensate by filling up as much time as possible pursuing tasks that will direct attention somewhere else; or, depending on the extent of emotional injury, attempt to put the past behind by locking the door to uninvited intruders, which then seem to come back all the more, apparently stronger. They will probably alternate between the two, but both moves are self-defeating. In the first case, the emotions are being denied, and in the second they are having their way; and it is not a matter of having to control them either, for the will that would overpower such feelings is negating itself in the process. Clearly, one is caught in a vicious circle, if the escape from reliving past experiences creates a dam effect where raw emotions build up until they burst through once more, and yielding grants them the power to dictate pain. An effective method of healing is required, and it lies in treading the middle path between active resistance and active succumbing. For one cannot eradicate from one's mind what has hitherto existed as part of one's emotional life, though the ego may fall into the trap of thinking so. Attempting such folly is akin to covering one's face with both hands before a mirror, peeping out only to see the image looking back at you, in short, pretending that it doesn't exist. In the inner regions of the unconscious where the hurt-provoking memories swarm (at least that is how the ego will tend to see them), the individual, when the pain is new and time has not yet begun to heal, must attempt to acknowledge the memories, for they increase the pain to the extent that escape is attempted — the surest way to be rid of hellfire is to become at one with it. This cryptic but wise saying suggests that far from incurring further suffering by becoming 'at one' with one's inner torment, it is not the memory itself that is destructive, but one's reaction to it.

Herein lies the conflict for the mortal in this situation, when past experience in the form of thoughts and images is fused with over-riding emotion that seems completely inseparable from it. Yet it is possible to detach the emotional reaction from the memory, and this is the sufferer's 'way out'; whenever such memories arise he or she must not allow themselves to be pulled in and immersed in its streams, but must sit on the banks and merely observe them as they pass. This means not taking part emotionally in the action, but simply 'watching' what goes on, for the individual must allow the memory to happen to them whilst resisting too much identification with it. Of course, this is easier said than done, but some comfort can be taken from the fact that one is dealing effectively with the problem since, Father Time notwithstanding, the wounds are going to heal much quicker this way than becoming caught up in the incessant burgeoning of the past. This method reduces the emotional impact of such memories, thus denying them the energy to evoke suffering; it is not the living with such memories that produces the conflict, it is the fear of opening the door to them. In admitting these elements of the past into consciousness, at least one has given up running away from oneself, and is effectively communicating the idea to the unconscious that, 'It's all right, I'm not afraid'. Like the body, the psyche is a self-repairing organ and (also in the same manner as the physical vehicle) to constrict the process will be expensive of both time and energy; offering resistance to a powerful memory simply keeps it alive which is defeating the object. It remains just as powerful when it re-asserts itself, and re-assert it will, for you will always remember something you are trying to forget.

For the individual who has suffered any painful encounter at the hands of fate and must now pay the price, visualisation will help to discover the road that leads to successful living, if the individual is ready for it. Emotional injury, as discussed above, must be adequately dealt with in order to clear the decks for the next phase, and the time of arrival of that next phase is determined by none other than the individual him or herself. It is during these periods of psychological instability that one discovers just how much life there is in one's veins, for the inner spirit or lust for life is something that defies even the attempts of depth psychology at classification. For precisely what is it deep within the individual being that makes him want to leap out of bed at 7:00 a.m., throw back the curtains and cheerfully announce, despite the freezing weather, 'Well, here's another morning, let's get on with it'? Then another will slide out from between the sheets at lunch time, wishing that the day would go away and that they didn't have to deal with the matter of existence. As is absurdly obvious, there is a remarkable difference between these two attitudes, but what is not obvious or even apparent is that both types possess the same inner potential, that access to the powers invested in the unconscious mind. The latter is unaware that the spirit so exuberantly manifested in the first individual secretly lies waiting to be discovered within themselves.

The process of retraining the emotions can be a lengthy one, since recovery from trauma and the efficacy of the healing process is entirely dependent on the individual caught up in it. Even when the sufferer has finally dealt with the shock, the expenditure of emotions and their assumed inner tormentors, and is marking out the route towards psychological health, he or she may still feel that the taste of life is conspicuously bland, finding little attraction to the things that once were a source of pleasure. When this happens the individual is unconsciously calling for a return of the spirit; the inner self is crying out for new life to be absorbed into it and needs the cooperation of the ego in order to effect the transformation. Terms such as 'spirit', 'life-force', 'libido' or 'psychic energy' are the most adequate representations available to the English language for that inner force which promotes the desire to entertain a rich and meaningful life, and there is evidence enough to suggest that it possesses actual physical properties, for example in bizarre photographs which reproduce images of the auras of living species, many of which look like the hallucinogenic visions of an artist laid down on canvas. Could these images be a reproduction of the heart and soul of animal and plant life?

Those who have thus become aware of the need to free the inner spirit in order to change the grey twilight of their existence into a brand new day full of possibilities must begin work on the inner self before they can expect a satisfying transformation to occur in their outer circumstances. Healing via mental images will effect the necessary changes and give the individual the opportunity to discover that the world waiting within holds many riches, that the life hitherto restrained in chains wants to be expressed, bearing in mind that some earnest desire is shown on the part of the individual. Without this the unconscious will simply continue to exercise the same old repetitive patterns as life becomes an imprisoning, slow death. If you will turn to Chapter Five, techniques are laid down for commencing the practice of visualisation: if you have identified with that individual living in the 'grey twilight' mentioned at the beginning of the paragraph, visualise yourself as inwardly content, projecting a confident, expressive personality, partaking in exciting or at least pleasurable ventures, delighting in the company of others, sharing laughter with friends, getting drunk and falling over. Whatever.

THE PHILOSOPHY OF VISUALISATION

The philosophy of visualisation, if one can call it that, hinges on the central idea that imagination tends to become material fact, since mind is all pervasive; not only in the physical self, the individual, the microcosm, but also in the cosmos, the universal, the macrocosm. And expressed in more straightforward terms, it is the age-old truth that whatever one can conceive with the imagination can be made into a reality through the use of the inner powers of the unconscious mind. In spite of such age-old maxims, the belief exists among many pseudospiritual types that the invocation of this interior power is meddlesome, and is forcing the universe into complying with demands which may not be in the subject's best interest because they interfere with his or her karma. We have heard much concerning the nature of karma ranging from the sublime to the ridiculous; either we are all of us on a quest for spiritual perfection and must reincarnate many times in order to achieve it (the only condition is, that if we misbehave whilst undertaking this journey, we must pay our dues in the next incarnation), or we will live our next life in the body of a species whose nature equals the way in which we have spent this life, say, a lower form of animal life. Thus, for those of us who do not wish to come back as next door's cat, it is essential to raise one's thoughts above the bestial instincts, strive to become more spiritual and lay off the tinned pilchards.

I have even heard the remark that, karmic interference aside, visualisation will only deliver effective results if the individual's karma actually allows them to happen, that is, if the mighty spiritual hierarchy (whatever that may be) will grant permission for the visualising to succeed. If that is the case, and I do not believe it to be so, then we are perpetually in the dark about our cherished dreams, and our aspirations and beliefs are rendered meaningless as we approach that elusive horizon, travelling without a shred of faith in the future. The way I see it, is that certain universal laws are present and whenever the offending mortal has violated any of them they must henceforth pay a penalty in exact proportion to the 'crime'. Now this does not mean to suggest a God who punishes an impotent human being for the transgression of a divine law circumscribed by the Holy Father alone. The real sin is ignorance of oneself and others and the sentences meted out range from bodily aches and pains to the horrors of loneliness and depression. Thus one's sufferances are a direct consequence of one's actions, a product of being out of sync with natural laws, not a punishment from Jehovah or the karmic results of having occupied the body of Vlad the Impaler in a past life. Perhaps the word 'law' is inappropriate when speaking of nature's processes for no actual regulations are imposed, it merely goes on unfolding and either we align with it, placing ourselves in harmony with whatever makes the universe spin (thus our own inner unfoldment), or we incur the kind of suffering mentioned above. The universe, God, fate, Mother Nature, or whatever, cannot be judged as either cruel or kind, good or evil, for it simply *is*. The great essayist Ralph Waldo Emerson remarks on this: 'All loss, all pain is particular; the universe remains to the heart unhurt. For it is only the finite that has wrought and suffered; the infinite lies stretched in smiling repose.'

Those who actively believe in the autonomy of the spiritual powers as if they resembled a panel of cosmic judges, perhaps see visualising for material objects and the like as interfering with the orderly processes of natural life but I believe this to be an inferior hand-spun philosophy, for the universe is not dogmatic, but pragmatic. By that I mean that nature, especially the simpler forms of life, does not have any specific ulterior motive for existing other than to exist, or perpetuate the birth–life–death cycle. It is pragmatic in the sense that its natural processes entail certain resultant effects, from the sea eroding pebbles on the beach into sand, to the repressed energy of the human being eventually erupting into self-destructive behaviour as they scream and spurt out a torrent of vengeful malice, ultimately aimed at no-one in particular. As is common, one is inclined to judge such behaviour as uncivilised and improper, blind to the fact that such rantings are an expression of something much deeper; angry emotions that are the natural consequence of repressed life energies which in no way intend to be held back — yet we castigate such maniacs. To emphasise the point, one would be less inclined to moralise about the vicious way that the wildlife on the plains of Africa is torn to shreds by the neighbouring lionesses. It's nature, we say. So if I were to give this spiritual hierarchy a consciousness (who presumably preside over the individual's karma), I would hear them saying: 'By all means go ahead and visualise and attract what you will, for that is your choice. But be aware of all that it entails, and to what it is you wish to become attached.' I would not, however, put the following words into their mouths: 'But you have not earned that thing which you desire and we are in no position to be able to grant it to you, no matter how much you visualise for it.'

So if we wanted to discover more of the relationship between the individual and the Universal Mind, we would have to find out the nature of the latter. What is Universal Mind? Firstly, we will have to make do with terminology like 'Cosmic Will', 'Infinite Intelligence', 'the hand of God', or 'way of all nature', because our language suffers from being unable to represent such a reality in any other way. From the human standpoint, it appears that nature has a will all of its own, albeit a cosmic one, as the hand of God steers us along the path without our direct knowledge, though this path is ultimately of our own making. Universal Mind appears to possess its own wisdom, and its will is that of moving forwards, silently engineering the unfoldment and development of natural life and we are required to grow with it, though this requirement does not stem from the decision of God. For example, the workings of this subtle power in the universe is paralleled in a much smaller version: the human body. A kind of intelligence is inherent in the physical vehicle when you consider the system of energy distribution and how it requires to be used up if one is to maintain a healthy balance. When an individual predisposed to a high level of physical or emotional energy refuses to express the needs of his or her body, perhaps through exercise, work, or more intimate kinds of expression, they are putting themselves out of harmony with the system and the body retaliates with aggravating tensions, frustration, headaches and the like. Yet what 'it' is that appears to have retaliated has only done so because the owner of it has violated a natural system which can only function properly with their cooperation. This is a paradigm which I feel suitably illustrates the nature of our relationship with the universe, an essence as part of the whole of life around us.

So it is almost as if there is something about life that requires to be lived and makes its demands on the human being, wanting to live through us, tempting us out into the light to participate in the great creator's handiwork; as has previously been noted by other writers, God needs man and woman just as much as they need God. From this standpoint we could assume that life would simply carry on evolving even without we mortals which, according to whose history lesson you sat in at school, is how it began. We take for granted the fact that plant life derives from a seed and that it is possible to discover how such organisms germinate and develop, but still have yet to see why. What is it about a certain kind of seed that enables it to burst forth into a horse-chestnut tree? Could it be its natural will, that of the Universal Mind itself, to grow, evolve and partake of life? Then, why are we here? To grow, evolve and partake of life? If that is the case, then our ability to create through visualisation seems like a necessary gift with which to have been blessed as we celebrate our approach to the future with forward looking aspirations and cherished dreams. Thus, I am inclined to reject the notion that visualisation is tampering with nature, for the cosmic will has the same idea in mind as any sincere visualiser — that of going forward.

On a more earthy level, being out of touch with the Universal Mind means a deviation from one's basic nature, either through ignorance or the demands of the environment. When this happens the disharmony is plainly expressed in the life of the individual: frustration of desire, poor relationships with others, over attachment to the past (frequently a source of pain) and those inexplicable little things that frequently go wrong, which when added up would amount to something quite big indeed. This is the unconscious trying to make itself heard and if the individual were to listen they would hear the voice telling them that these constant mistakes are symptomatic of the mismanagement of choice. And here 'choice' is the keyword: for example, many love relationships suffer because of the frequent, if not serious, disagreements and annoyances that arise. This syndrome is an unconscious rumbling which is trying to tell both partners something about themselves; obviously something is not working, yet both partners have the choice to deal with the matter and with enough serious effort, the chance to correct the situation. The man in this predicament, for example, will either not bother making the effort to look at the problem, which simply aggravates it, or he will decide on a course of action that may be entirely inappropriate for the cure of the situation. The latter case implicitly states that we cannot always be sure of making the right choices, but at least we can first examine our motives for making that choice, but often even having done that and acted on our decision proves to be no remedy. This is the case when the problem cannot be dealt with in the object, for the problem lies within the man himself.

Looking inward to discover ourselves saves many hurt feelings and our lives and relationships run smoother as a result; this is what is meant by being in tune with the Cosmic Will, but the effort to express what is down there must also be made. There is a case well known to me of a relationship which contained many of these unconscious stirrings which were evidence that all was not well in the interaction of the two partners. The male half, whom I shall call Ben, simply refused to broaden his focus and see that the accompanying niggles and lack of real communication were compounded by his approach to the relationship. Ben is the caring and considerate type and this is exactly the underlying reason for most of the problems which arose, and on the face of it, it is quite paradoxical. But our lives cannot express harmony if we do not try to understand others too, and Ben made no attempt to peer beyond the veil of his girlfriend's apparent nature: she found his goody-goody approach quite suffocating, and it became obvious that if he wanted to remain attractive to her, which he did, he would need to express more dynamic, forceful energies. If he had simply been more self-assertive, then the relationship would have run much more smoothly and dare I say, naturally. For the blending of these two natures would only be harmonious with an equal expression of that lively, ebullient energy which we describe as 'fiery', for Alison is indeed a fiery type, which required some heat on the part of Ben for their relationship to survive. Or so it turned out.

That Ben was unconscious of such fiery energies in himself is excusable, but his reluctance to see the reality of the situation, prominently staring him in the face (and the friends around him too) is quite simply sad. As it transpired, with Alison's continuing disillusionment and belief that it was hopeless, it was not long before the unconscious intervened and engendered the obvious situation, the end of Ben and Alison. In retrospect, it is easy to see when part of one's life is off-course, though that course is not determined from the start, since Ben could easily have made different choices that resulted in a much more graceful flow for his relationship. It is when we strenuously resist this flow of life, because things are not turning out as we would like, that it becomes impossible to effect a satisfactory change and the old vicious circle looms on the horizon yet again.

The deepest layers of the unconscious partake of the qualities of Universal Mind since there is a secret-soul in each human with the instinctive motivation towards the living of life itself, most commonly manifest in those restless individuals we call lively, spirited, energetic. For what is it in us, that thing that may hardly ever be contemplated, egging us on to dream fabulous dreams that may one day be made into reality, clothing us with ideals about Utopian bliss, nirvana, world peace, or simply the intention to live a full and prosperous life? The natural course of Universal Mind attempts to mark out its path and be expressed through every individual. Its intelligence can be perceived by those willing enough to listen and thus see its principle expressed in their lives. Visualisation is the augmentor of fabulous dreams, putting the human being in touch with innermost desires, permitting visions of that better day to come, accentuating that yearning felt deep down inside which is religious in quality. The notion that there is meaning and purpose to life springs from this same well, carrying the individual through even their darkest hour when that sense of meaning has become dimmed. Mental imagery turns cloudy awareness of the inner spirit into a bright recognition, spurring us on to live life, put heart and soul into the powers within, for having set our hearts on something we are halfway there already.

CHAPTER 2
INNER LANDSCAPES —
THE NATURE OF
THE IMAGE

Were those Olympian deities not represented pictorially and given both human and divine attributes, there would never have been the possibility of understanding of what is now called the unconscious.

A good painter is to paint two main things, namely men and the workings of a man's mind.
Leonardo Da Vinci

In these things I have seen
Dreams inflicted upon me
When the snarling dog is rested
When the angry ocean leaves

When the eye is taken over
To show what fantasy means
Then restless visions arise
In the heart of one who needs

And you make your dreams so real
Though life offers its chaos to you
You will never take no for an answer
At each terrible turn of the screw

For you know even turning a corner
Into different streets you may know
Is to step on the wheel of fortune
The card that you picked long ago. *Capri*

The purpose of this chapter is to inspire in the reader the imaginative faculties necessary for the promotion of visual scenarios, to be performed in mental imaging rituals. Consider the above poem; its romantic emphasis on visions, fantasies and dreams and the impassioned longings of the protagonist whose 'snarling dog' is the intense, feverish desire nature that stubbornly refuses to lie down. These lines resonate far stronger in the human heart than do the usual, rather clipped, forms of expression one is used to in describing something, for poems, songs and many types of fiction bypass the conventional, linear structure of language, which must at all times make sense and be 'correct'. They manage to express much more about the human condition by virtue of colourful phrases, expansive gestures, lengthy surreal allusions and nonsense lines: the intuition understands them totally, for it makes its own sense out of them.

In the third verse we find the subject projecting visions, waiting for the chance to see them materialise despite whatever life serves up and with each painful 'turn of the screw', we are to assume that his life at present is not a pretty sight. The writer alludes to the emotions triggered off when the dynamic world of images is entertained, though with the poem's elemental passions, it is unlikely to be referring to the use of these images for ephemeral daydreaming. The card chosen long ago is simultaneously selected by him and chosen for him (a metaphor for the free will/fate dilemma), for his choice to climb on to the wheel of fortune will result in a fate peculiar to the time he steps on it, i.e. whatever is happening then in his unconscious. But then it can be argued that the time was chosen for him, which brings destiny back into it. Either way, I believe that the paradox is resolved in the maxim that one calls forth one's fate by the exercising of free will. In this respect, the two are not mutually exclusive. Before we veer away from the point, in their entirety the verses portray the individual's intent to create through the powers of mind and the subject's understanding of the apparently spontaneous laws governing fate. Or maybe you interpret it quite differently? Maybe other impressions occur to you as you read it?

In the same manner, paintings of the great masters, classic symphonies, erotic sculpture, imaginatively penned literature, Shakespearian sonnets and the like, are invested with the capacity to dance with the emotions of anyone who cares enough to respond, for they speak directly to the heart, words that the intellect cannot hear. It is this same non-fragmented response, like becoming transfixed gazing upon a beautiful woman or man, that catalyses the necessary moods in visualisation, for as we shall see, ambience and image are the tools of the unconscious. One particular outgrowth of this non-worded, free flowing aspect of communication is the symbol — in itself an abstract item, a concept, until one suffuses it with a facet of life, giving it a life of its own. The symbol serves to amplify a hidden meaning which cannot be reached by taking it at face value, and always stands just between subjective consciousness and the object to which it is relating, and in representing a particular form of inner experience in this way, it allows the individual to tune in on his or her own particular wavelength. In a way which adjectives never can, the symbol roundly describes subjective experience for it arouses and amplifies emotional response, in contrast to the intellect, which often cuts the meaning short.

For instance, symbolism is most effective when applied to the intangible world of human psychology: when it represents emotions such as love, hate, anger, excitement, jealousy; when it portrays motivations from the inside like the effort at self-knowledge, searching for love, ambition or the need to relate to others. Common adjectives used to describe certain emotional states — miserable, elated, in love, enthusiastic — are at best a label and succeed only in drawing up a rather flat interpretation of something dynamically alive and full of energy. So the psyche expresses life through symbols, because all mental processes cannot adequately represent nature itself, especially feeling states drawn from the unconscious.

By way of example, how are we to come to an understanding of the meaning of 'peacefulness', the experience thereof, in such a way that its full implications are explored? Worded labels will not suffice, for they can only represent one facet of the whole, but a symbol that suggests peace or calmness allows the individual to respond with a host of subjective associations that renders its meaning clear — to the individual, that is. For symbols are full of meaning, and we will always identify with them in our own particular fashion: agents of evil forces such as Lucifer, Dionysus, Pan, are not regarded as quite so evil in some quarters of the human kingdom. They symbolise the cthonic urge that acts as the natural complement to the higher, civilised self, and cannot be condemned as sinful because that is another way of avoiding having to deal with human nature. To return to the example, a sense of inner calm and stability is commonly symbolised in the gentle dove, The Garden of Eden, the idyllic countryside or rosily secure family unit, as the unconscious clothes its contents in the language of imagery and projects them outwards. For an emotion or mood must take form if one is to draw meaning from it at a conscious level, thus the psyche produces the allegory, metaphor or analogy as a mode of communication in either a pictorial or lyrical construction.

A client once described depression as a blackened, frightening tunnel, inhabited by hostile creatures that hid in the darkness watching his every move. I did not question him further about the tunnel and its hideous specimens, presumably there to taunt or even attack him, because I grasped the implications of this picture immediately. He went on to paint a rather gloomy scene of darkness and decay as he was forced to go through the tunnel, not knowing how long it would last until reaching the light at the other end. The forbidding passage was something he had to venture through, an unavoidable fate, since the lingering effects of intense depression do not disappear overnight. Thus, it was envisaged as a journey he was called upon to undertake, to work through his pain whilst encountering the figures just below the threshold of consciousness that terrified him so much. These creatures are personifications of emotional chaos which threaten to invade consciousness, frenziedly tearing up the secure roots of the ego and swelling the mind with an orgy of pain and destruction. My client's unconscious produced these images as symbolic manifestations of what was happening 'down there'; had he attempted an intellectual analysis of this experience, the depth of emotion with all of its subtle ramifications could never have been adequately conveyed.

The mind's susceptibility to visual and emotional language is demonstrated in the phenomenon of commercial advertising, for its power to convince means that the suggestible houseperson returns from the supermarket with items that he or she would not usually consider purchasing. For when it is suggested to our emotions that we would indeed benefit from washing powder that can actually work in cold water, the body spray that causes men to chase after you waving a bunch of flowers, or the instant meal in a carton that actually tastes like the ingredients listed on the label, we are often content to swallow the suggestion whole. The plethora of TV advertisements spoon fed to us in our living rooms each day acts like a mild drug on the unconscious of the observer, like a kind of semi-hypnotism. However, this is not intended as a gripe about advertising, rather to show that the mind responds quite readily to visual suggestion as it absorbs the hypnotic charm of the commerical break.

HEROES AND HEROINES

Our responses of either warmth or coldness, compassion or disgust, amazement or incredulity, are reflections of emotional attunement to a given person or situation. When we discover a kindred feeling with the tragic heroes of fiction or classical myth, when we identify with the misery of the spurned lover, or the delight of the victor at conquering his ruthless enemy, some other kind of language resonates within us. We have, at some time or other, associated some of our personal experience with the protagonist of fictional literature, song lyrics or the silver screen; it is at these moments that we see some of ourselves in them: when the words of a song are talking about us, when the narrative of a story is identical to events from our past and the uncanny feeling arises that it was written specially for us. Whether we identify with a Joe Lampton, Scarlett o'Hara, Captain Bligh, Romeo or Juliet, or even Bet Lynch, the various plights of such characters represent aspects of our own testing trials through the maze of life. Mythology offers a wealth of material portraying humankind's earliest chafing against fate and the trials that must be endured on the road ahead in the form of the hero or heroine, symbols for the motivations of the conscious ego. Often, a hero figure is pitted against one of the gods, a representation of unconscious elements in the human psyche, and from this standpoint the mortal and immortal figures symbolise aspects of the conscious and unconscious mind respectively. The tale of Icarus, from ancient Greece, is a mythologised portrayal of a particular fact of psychic life, and through its apparent simplicity can be gleaned meanings lying deep within its framework so that it no longer remains a simple example of ancient story telling.

The myth makes reference to the fragile human ego and how easily it is deflated or crushed through a personal mistake or a rejection by others. The list is endless for there is an infinite number of situations in which an over-inflated sense of self takes a battering, in which pride goes before a fall. Icarus' father, Daedalus, had constructed wings for himself and his son in order to make good their escape from the Labyrinth where the Minotaur was imprisoned. The wings were secured with wax on a framework that when strapped to their arms enabled them to soar high into the clouds. However Icarus was overcome with the thrill of his new found ability to fly and continued to ascend higher towards the heavens. Similarly, when life is sweet, we are tempted to believe that nothing can ever go wrong, that the whole world is at our fingertips and ready to do our bidding. Like Daedalus' son, we bask in the limelight of our new found power in a direct assumption that our fortune is the work of the conscious ego. But as time has told us, nature demands a compensation, a balance of power whereby the ego must acknowledge a force greater than its own, and that must take place sooner or later. Icarus flew so high that the heat of the sun began to melt the wax securing the feathers allowing him to fly, and one by one they came off until the mortal hero could no longer stay in the air, and without his artificial support he came crashing down into the sea.

This particular incident, which is part of a much larger story, contains so many symbolic ramifications that one could continue at length suggesting what the contents of the tale might imply. Generally, in myth, the protagonist symbolises the individual ego, and the direction thereof, whilst the surrounding characters represent other aspects of the psyche, either conscious or unconscious. Daedalus can be seen here as the unconscious inner voice of authority, for indeed he warns Icarus not to fly too near the sun. That the feathers are attached with wax alludes to the fragility of the human ego and how vulnerable it proves when expanded out of regular proportion; it is as if by its act of inflation, with a kind of bloated pride, it calls upon forces outside the self that are inimical to it. The sun is a symbolic image of the potential god-alikeness within man, that which grants him the power to create. Icarus placed himself on the same divine level as the creator as he approached the sun, the consequence of which was his fall down to earth. This myth has been enacted throughout history by those despotic individuals who, in meddling with the gods, engineered their own downfall through superimposing on to the ego an omnipotence which did not rightly belong there. People, like Hitler, who ascended to positions of enormous power had to answer to the Fates because of their abuse of that power. Either they did not possess the intelligence to use it creatively, or simply believed that they were God. At the climax of the Bellorophon/Chimaera myth, which has the same psychological implications as the Icarus tale, Zeus is supposed to have remarked, 'So perish all those who seek to rival the gods.'

It is not only in the stories of mortals, gods and monsters of mythology that one can discover symbolic themes at work. Fairy tales too can perform this demonstration, in fact any larger than life tale with a quest, where the hero must do battle with an opponent and sometimes rescue a fair maiden from the clutches of a formidable foe *en route* to his destination, may be utilised in this way. More modern fictional examples contain the same motifs, for example, *Lost Horizon* (which is the subject of the following section), a vivid portrayal of the inner quest for wholeness, spiritual values and the beauty of the soul, where the chief character finds himself in a landscape reflecting the total harmony of his inner self. But before we move on, let us summarise the chief archetypal figures and their symbolic meanings: the Hero/Heroine (the principal motivations of consciousness, the individual ego); Gods/Goddesses (masculine/feminine forces at work in the unconscious that are rendered godlike owing to our being out of touch with them); the Enemy/ Villain (elements of our inferior nature which we try to hide and which thus function unconsciously); the enchanting female (feminine elements of the male psyche which he sees in the woman but nevertheless are part of him; the reverse is true in heroine myths where she encounters male characters).

SHANGRI-LA

The thoroughly imaginative, romantic fantasy *Lost Horizon* appears on the surface to be no more than that, yet beyond the narrative is an archetypal motif running through human nature, that of an idealistic quest for that elusive, personal haven where peace and prosperity reign always under the benevolent rule of a loving god. As in myth, this inner odyssey is projected onto a material landscape, with the accompanying characters and locations representing elements of the psyche that may be inadequately described in words alone. The original film version in 1931 (a remake was released in the early 1960s) is a lavish production that allures the imagination of anyone prepared to wholly involve themselves in its fantasy. Moreover, seen from the symbolic viewpoint (as employed in the psychologies of scholarly writers like James Hillman, Ean Begg and Edward Whitmont), it presents a thorough picture of the living psyche. The central figure, Conway, a twentieth-century version of the mythological hero, takes the viewer on a journey through inner space, the conscious and unconscious minds. These are skilfully represented as the competitive and materialistic Western world where ego clashes and striving for a piece of the action are the usual diet, and a curious exotic paradise in the East where the values of the West are thrown into reverse with an ambience of tranquility, a respect for the beauties of nature and the powers she holds. The strange quietude of Shangri-La, populated by its semi-immortal residents, is a powerful symbol of the unconscious in its beneficial aspect; one can experience such a place in meditation, in night-time dreams, in states of total relaxation, and of course not least in creative visualisation.

The hero, Conway, accompanied by his brother and three other passengers, is returning from the Orient by aeroplane when it is discovered that a bogus pilot, some oriental mystery gentleman, happens to be at the control panel in place of the appointed pilot. Even at this early stage in the story, it is notable that Conway refuses to challenge the substitute pilot despite protests from his colleagues (whom I shall consider as attendant elements of consciousness), almost as if he knows to where they are heading. If Conway is the central ego figure of the psyche, then his brother George, the two other male attendants (one self-effacing and neurotic, the other, imposing and rude) and the only female member of the party symbolise elements of consciousness that are in conflict with the intentions of the ego, yet nevertheless co-exist within the same individual. Like Conway, we may hold noble ideas and aspirations and set ourselves upon a path towards attaining them, yet we still hear the all too audible whispers of doubt, unexpressed resentment, and the suggestion of our own inferiority. In *Lost Horizon* they are portrayed as fleshly caricatures in the individuals who accompany Conway to Shangri-La.

After having landed amidst the slopes of Tibet, they are led to the inscrutable Mr Chang, the gracious host of Shangri-La, a kind of Himalayan Billy Butlin. As befits the mythical theme, Conway is the single member of the travelling party who is not intimidated by this new environment. As it later transpires, he has been summoned there by the High Llama himself (a symbol for the spiritual state of non-self that can be reached through deep meditation). Mr Chang, whose countenance evokes that of an aged, worldly-wise guru possessed of the wisdom of the ages, symbolises the voice sounded by the unconscious to which we must listen when it makes its unverbalised tones heard. This is not quite as abstruse as it first sounds since that voice, the mouthpiece of the unconscious, is the same one that provides the right solutions to pressing problems that refused to be resolved under the direction of the conscious mind, that acts as an oracle for the uninspired musical composer who, having tired of his efforts of writing, hears a flurry of notes in his head and knows that they are the right ones to use in the manuscript. The voice makes its presence felt in other ways too, as to the person who, without apprehending why, knows that someone close is in trouble and needs assistance, so he returns home to find his wife hysterically in tears. That this guide can provide answers on request then comes as no surprise, but we need to ask the question in the right way, for it is only when conscious control is relaxed that the inner voice can be heard and it becomes the vehicle of immensely valuable information. In *Lost Horizon*, it is the indignant George and his two male companions (for the girl rarely expresses herself) who ask Mr Chang the wrong questions such as, 'How soon do we get out of here?' for which he provides rather unsatisfactory answers. The question that they are required to ask is simply, 'Why?'

These three characters, not realising that they are in Conway's unconscious are at a loss to yield direct answers from the guide, and in like manner when we find ourselves confronted with uncomfortable moods, especially in periods of depression over which we have little control, the ego asks in desperation, 'How long will it last?'. If the unconscious could verbalise an answer like the benign Mr Chang, it would say, 'Don't try running away from it, try to understand it, then there will be no need to run.'

The seeker Conway exemplifies this necessity to understand the workings of the unconscious as he asks Chang about the general way of life in Shangri-La. Settling on the question of religion, he asks which particular one is practised. 'Moderation in all things,' replies the guide, which is another way of expressing the unconscious urge towards a balance and the maintaining of equilibrium.

ATTRACTION OF OPPOSITES

The theme of compensation pervades nature both individually and collectively through that phenomenon we have called the attraction of the opposites: lean too far over to one side, in thought or action, and the stage is set for nature to bring about a compensatory action. An over emphasis on one particular mode of behaviour invariably attracts others who will resist you, or at least play black to your white, cold to your warmth, and cynical to your innocent, for the man (or woman) shaped with an unbending inflexible nature is paralysed to the extent that he is unable to deal with the personalities of those whom he unconsciously draws upon himself. This psychological phenomenon is extrapolated into the collective when enacted as the reaction to, for example, political leaders, the doctrines of religion, the tenets of certain heavy-handed philosophers and at a less sublime level, popular trends in modern culture. For every government in power there exists an opposition party; for every number of saints, a large proportion of sinners; for those who subscribe to the work of that maestro of sufferance, Nietzsche, there are those who will adhere to the happiness philosophy of William James, and every bible thumper who stands on the town hall square administering directives for the Christian way of life draws to himself, a proportion of spectators who find his remarks not only laughable, but virulent. In today's prevailing fashions one also finds this phenomenon at work. As soon as one particular group or movement gathers momentum, another group with quite different tastes swings directly to the opposite extreme, as if to preserve the balance. Where one finds the night time trendy set with their addiction to glamour and making an impression, one may find not so far away, the opposition who insist on being 'natural' and prefer the company of a close friend, the log fire of the country pub and a bottle of brown ale. It occurred in the early sixties when the immaculate, pretty-boy image of the Beatles ushered in the new trend for pop groups, until a new band of long haired monsters called the Rolling Stones appeared as the direct antithesis to this all too perfect, clean shaven icon. I am not describing the actual groups in themselves, but the image which the public wove around them; America and England made gods out of the Beatles but nature resented this and set five mischievous vagabonds against them. As Tom Wolfe's rather bloated PR announcement puts it, 'The Beatles want to hold your hand, but the Stones want to burn your town.' Anyway, it's time to return to Shangri-La.

We last left Conway in conversation with the guide Chang in our symbolic portrayal of the unconscious, who informs our hero that crime is non-existent in Shangri-La since no-one ever lacks anything and thus there is no need to steal what rightly belongs to someone else. Crime, as Chang points out, is the consequence of lack but since there is no lack here, there is no need for any judicial law. One may experience a similar abundance, rich in potential, lying in wait in the unconscious, in visualisation where no limits are placed on the individual. During waking consciousness where the mind is busy dealing with its impressions it is harder to imagine those big dreams as attainable, thus the need to go downstairs in the silence to draw on the reserves of the inner mind, for the soul can conceive of things that the ego cannot.

As the story progresses, our hero is granted an audience with his higher spiritual self, symbolised in the almost spectral figure of the High Llama, after much soul searching and self interrogation. As it transpires, the High Llama needs Conway to assume responsibility for the running of Shangri-La and as far as the narrative is concerned, this is simply because the old man is at last going to die and Conway is the man he has been waiting for. But interpreted at a symbolic level it suggests something quite different: the higher spiritual self requires Conway's attentiveness and cooperation if it is ever to manifest and fulfil the expressions of potential life housed within, and in return, as the Llama promises, it has 'lots to offer'. Quiet communion with the inner forces often taps great psychological resources which cannot be summoned in any other way; during one particular scene in the film Conway's brother George aggressively confronts a female resident about 'getting out of here', and she simply runs away. When we rail against nature and vigorously strain for the answer to a problem, it defiantly eludes us and as the story later illustrates, it is this persistence of the ego that creates a wearisome, pathetic struggle for Conway as the shadow of doubt eclipses his inherent faith. On the one hand, he rests assured that he has discovered his true dream, yet on the other sits the notion that it is simply too good to be true, an empty sham dressed up as paradise.

Brother George thoroughly rejects these new surroundings and begins to chafe against them, like so many sceptics who will deny the validity of thought power, though the other three characters have since fallen in love with the opulent Shangri-La and have decided to remain. Conway has meanwhile gone one better and begun an intense love-affair with a Shangri-La damsel who might well be described as the archetypal sweet young thing: easy on the eye, slim, dark, petite, straight out of an advertisement for French stockings. It is she who suggests to Conway, whilst he cannot quite bring himself to explain why Shangri-La is so familiar, that perhaps a part of him has always belonged here. Even in the midst of this blessed, unspoiled existence, distant rumblings are at work that will throw Conway into the very jaws of disaster. It is later on that he finds himself locking horns with his brother (who has devised an escape route that comprises of rescuing a girl resident) in open conflict about the apparent unreality of Shangri-La and the lies that seem to be hidden behind Chang's mask of sincerity and wisdom. The girl, who also desires to be free of her prison, has made contact with the band of nomads who had first shepherded Conway's party there, and it is with their guidance through the forbidding routes in the mountains that they will make their escape. The conversion for Conway arrives when, after listening to accusations about Chang from the girl, the seed of disbelief takes root and he begins to entertain his doubts. Here we find a not uncommon dilemma: the doubt that strikes a hammer blow at the last minute when having been virtually assured of success, in whatever form, we do a U-turn on the path we have set out upon. Conway will go with his brother.

This doubting traitor within, the resistance to journeying into the unknown, is a common cause of failure for many individuals. How many times have we abandoned our ambitious projects through having decided in advance that it will not be successful, in false satisfaction that we would be better off without it and the extra effort? Conversely, there are times when, after a little hesitation, we decide to venture into unfamiliar territory and discover to our surprise that something is there for us and we are glad that we acted upon our decision. The same could not be said however for Conway who, with his lover chasing after him to no avail, embarks on the journey homewards with his brother and female cohort who, as it later turns out, starts to age so rapidly that she dies. For several days the two of them, now devoid of the assistance of the porters, struggle through hazardous mountain passes, running the gauntlet amid the hostile, snowy blizzards of the Himalayas. This evokes a symbolic scene of the frail ego left to its own devices, for having abandoned his friendship with the unconscious, Conway must rely on the uncertainty of will power in order to conquer the elements.

The next fate to befall Conway is the premature end of his brother. George falls to his death from a sheer drop and as Conway watches helplessly, the gods claim another victim. However, as is befitting the nature of all good heroic quests, Conway eventually finds his way back to his beloved Shangri-La, though not until after an extensive, punishing struggle. His lapse of faith accentuates the desire to recapture his dream, for which he must first find the appropriate path, in this case literally and metaphorically. At the climax of his dance with death, Conway is found unconscious, but still alive, by a Chinese mission sent to recover him whilst his associates await his return in England. It is whilst sailing home that his memory returns, after a temporary spell of amnesia, and he jumps overboard to begin once again, the perilous excursion to the Eden-like Shangri-La, only this time more frantically than ever, for he knows what is to be found there.

This celebration of imaginative story telling captures an archetypal theme pervading collective psychology, in this case the inner search for meaning, a personal heaven, a re-entry into Eden. Typically it is projected onto an exterior landscape whereby the inward, intangible quest becomes an actual physical journey. The image-making faculty is so powerful in the human being that we create living caricatures too of those around us and amplify only the qualities that we wish to see. That this function occurs unconsciously ought to come as no surprise, for we would rather believe inwardly that certain qualities exist in the other person, particularly in emotional relationships, than acknowledge that they are most often the creations of our own minds. However, some of these mental creations are going to be realised under the direction of the conscious mind, for they form the blueprint of dreams we intend to see manifest in bricks and mortar, when the image shall become flesh.

DREAM TIME

For this section I will resist the temptation to provide a general menu of dream interpretations, for experience has shown that the cut-and-dried methods as employed in dream dictionaries usually fail miserably in that the revelations they provide are most often quite unrelated to the dreamer. No single manual of the so-called meanings of particular dreams can ever possess a comprehensive scheme that applies wholly to one individual, for as is so often the case, the interpretations are laden with fatalistic weight, done in a style that evokes the prognostications of the fortune teller at a village fête. *The* authentic book of fate is being written in one's own psyche by none other than

46

oneself and it is possible to read into some of its pages even as it is being written, for dreams replay to the individual what is going on in the unconscious at the time. The study of dreams, like an education in the tarot deck, involves a prior knowledge of the general meanings of the symbols produced by the dream, notwithstanding the ability to intuit their meaning at a personal level. I have already exemplified various archetypal motifs in the myth and fiction of historical literature, and these same quests reappear in the life of twentieth-century people under different names and in modern disguises, not least in their night-time sleep states. As mythographer Joseph Campbell put it: 'The latest incarnation of Oedipus, the continued romance of Beauty and the Beast stands this afternoon on the corner of Forty-second street . . . waiting for the traffic lights to change.'

Thus, the aim of this section is to raise the issue of what those apparently unrelated and weird images might mean within the context of the dream, and how they relate to the subject's waking life, for the former is saying something about the latter. As we wade through a landscape redolent of the trip in 'Lucy In The Sky With Diamonds', we discover a world of disconnected, usually unrelated characters and settings that have been pieced together in such a preposterous way that the ego must describe them as weird. The unconscious has clothed itself in pictorial form with a seemingly random array of meaningless images; that there can be an infinite number of situations, and a similarly infinite number of arrangements of them, is why the static, one-line interpretations in literature on dreams prove to be inadequate. Chetwynd's *Dictionary for Dreamers* (see Bibliography) is the most useful study I have found so far, for even though it is arranged in the format of a dictionary, it mostly suggests, rather than categorically asserts, what the various symbols mean, the interpretations having been based on the universal meanings of the symbols as they have applied throughout our history.

By way of example, dreaming of taking a journey, regardless of the means of transport, is interpreted as the metaphorical journey through life itself. For instance, young people in the process of establishing themselves in the material world often dream of travelling to unfamiliar locations, unsure of their destinations, with unlikely travelling companions. Even the one basic theme of travelling contains many different ramifications: there is the means of transport (car, aeroplane, boat, train, bus) and who may happen to be driving; the number of passengers *en route*; whether the vehicle is moving fast or slow; whether one is departing or arriving; the narrative of the dream and the situations one notices most readily. It can be seen that, with hindsight, the aforementioned are themselves symbolic of some aspect of the dreamer, so it is worth taking into consideration as many details as one can recall on waking.

The following example of a serial dream, i.e. several dreams related to one another as the individual passes through a particular phase of events in waking life, portrays the way in which the unconscious sheds meaningful images that represent the condition of the psyche at the present time. It demonstrates how the mind, having digested an experience, arbitrarily translates unconscious energies into pictorial language, some of it heart-warming, some of it fragmented and seemingly non-sensical, some of it desperate and frightening. In this particular instance we have a series of dreams that depict the transformation at work within the unconscious of a client of mine who wanted his birth chart interpreted, whilst suffering the emotional shock of his marriage break up. And during his progress from heartbreak case to an individual who eventually gained inner strength and resilience, he was able to dispel painful memories and cherish new hopes and aspirations for the future. The first dream occurred a few days after the break up:

> I am in the upstairs section of an old uninhabited building when
> I suddenly hear a loud explosion and I am aware that the
> building is going to collapse. Part of the floor is missing and I
> can see through to the room below. Some of the floor though is

very thin and I kick through it making the hole much bigger. It was like I wanted to make the hole more enlarged to see what was below. On the lower level are two cats, and one of them runs away as if it is frightened.

I felt as if my client knew deep inside, the full implications of the 'blast' and his voluntary destruction of certain rigid attitudes which were preventing him from seeing what might be 'down there'. The dream was portraying what was housed in his psyche and the necessary annihilation of certain contents that must take place prior to the rebirth of new life energies. The house was dilapidated and about to crumble, something to which my client relates the state of his marriage prior to the split, but the dream is really saying something about his attitude to the relationship. The consequent emptiness he felt is symbolised in the desolation and emptiness of the house. The old structures upon which he had erected his life were no longer supportive and had fallen into disrepair. Indeed he acknowledges this, for in the dream he kicks through the floor to the lower level of the building in assistance of the destruction.

After we had discussed the dream, I suggested that he use visualisation as a means of self-healing and emotional repair and to my surprise, he had already acquired sufficient knowledge and experience of the art to be able to practise it effectively. At that point I offered an interpretation on the two cats seen in the unconscious: I suggested they symbolised his inner resourcefulness and cunning that if put to use would be of enormous help. There still remained, though, some self-doubt and fear, quite naturally enough, since one of the cats in the dream had run away. It was two weeks before I saw him again and to my great delight he had been using visualisation almost religiously, perhaps to attract a new partner, but whatever it was he was employing the technique for, the unconscious was responding positively. Here is the dream he recalled:

I am going upstairs into a flat which belongs to my grandmother. The living room has just been redecorated because of fire damage, then I see a young man, the decorator, receiving payment from my grandmother. Then I see that the metal frame surrounding the gas fire has also been painted, and that the paint is still wet. The fire is turned on also.

As my client patiently assisted in the inner healing of wounded emotions, the dream demonstrated that his unconscious was indeed being 'redecorated' with fresh paint although the new look was not yet complete, for the fire, which to my client symbolised the heat of inner suffering, continues to burn through the paint. Therefore the burning continues alongside the work performed on the unconscious with mental imagery. The young decorator, symbolising the ego's efforts, is being rewarded for his work by an older female relative, his inner 'female' wisdom. Thus does the dream offer hope: his efforts at transforming his inner state were being repaid in some way as he slowly came to terms with his inner centre and continued to infuse new images into the unconscious. He experienced the following dreams several weeks later:

I find myself in a park, walking close to the railings surrounding it. My attention is focused on a row of houses that overlooks the area where I am walking, and one of the houses stands out from the rest because of the repair work recently done on it. Part of the house has been rebuilt with new bricks.

I follow a friend's mother into the hallway of their house and then she seems to disappear. I am standing at the entrance to the living room but I do not go in. The living room is not occupied but I do notice that it is elegantly furnished with glamorous items like silk cushions and velvet drapes.

My client's series of dreams, of which the above two are both enlightening and optimistic, continued to express the unconscious life as a sequence of structures that contain various energies, and as the dream illustrates, the repair work is nearly complete and the interior has been revived with exquisite furnishing. The attractiveness of the living room suggests that whatever is down there has since become more healthy and palatable to the ego. Thus did his outward life take on a similar appearance as the inner healing took place, for whatever is the quality of one's external world is merely a manifestation of interior potential.

CHAPTER 3
CREATION IN MIND —
IF YOU HAVE FAITH

One is driven to that which one seeks by an almost reverent feeling that, once born, cannot be destroyed. It is kept to oneself, safe from the unbelief of others, safe from the reach of those who would steal it. For one who keeps faith locked in the heart has no real need to venture too far in search of desires, for at the same time they will be out there seeking that desirous heart.

An exhortation containing similar words of enlightenment to this chapter's title is recorded in the Bible (Matthew, 17:20), and though it is not my intention to use Christian gospel to validate my ideas in any way, despite its religious overtones, the message holds a significance in a psychological sense. Faith is a way of being which generates positive results in the area to which it is applied, and my work as an astrologer has shown me that each individual uses this archetypal motivation in a particular arena of life. But the individual uses it unconsciously, that is, the word 'faith' and its attendant meanings is more likely never considered and he or she operates under this kind of belief without consciously realising it — and is lucky. This confident expectation about life which I would define as unconscious yielding or letting go, is in many ways the harbinger of an abundant, meaningful, ultimately successful way of life. It is the faith in things not yet manifest, the mentality that can say with absolute conviction that it's bound to happen sooner or later, the knowledge, absent of facts and details, that trusts in life and knows that good things will come to pass, the unshakeable conviction that there is someone up there, or more likely, down there, acting as guide and mentor, looking after me. For the Christian, that protective figure is the Father, The Lord God Almighty; for the depth psychologist it is the unconscious.

The faith one places in God to grant personal wishes is no different in kind from the trusty visualiser's debt to the unconscious forces. Consequently, for the power to be released into the universe, one must relinquish the battle between ego and circumstance, lay down arms and surrender. One only needs to notice, in the lives of so many people, the phenomenon whereby the goal which they had so ardently sought came about when they had at last given in and ceased to struggle. It is almost as if their attempts to secure by conscious volition were the very things debarring them from attainment; then, from out of the blue as they retire in apparent defeat, lo and behold do they find what they are looking for. Is this the response to one's prayers or the enigmatic workings of unconscious mind? Whichever way one approaches the answer, there exists a reciprocal action from the universe that cannot be ignored and which is immutable, and whether one rails hysterically at life, shaking a fist towards the heavens at an imaginary being, withdraws into sorrowful brooding in the privacy of one's mind, or conversely gazes into the sun towards that same imaginary being, possessed of an inexplicable sense of fullness and joy, one can only expect the universe to react accordingly.

So what is faith? What does it do for you? Is it some magical force available only to the initiated? Such a simple message as is the title of this chapter would cause a few raised eyebrows from the many inveterate rationalists it has been my good fortune to encounter. I will discuss their arguments in the section on attraction. Faith, in the office of creative visualisation is like having all of the lights turned up full, a glowing confident feeling that one's prayers could be answered at any moment. If this is beginning to sound too fantastic for words, it is only because modern humanity has placed so much reliance on tangible reality that it becomes almost impossible to have faith in that which has not yet happened, in a lifestyle that has yet to be evolved. Nor can faith truly be represented in intellectual terms for it is essentially an emotion, an inner support system on which to base operations in the external world augmented by the assurance that one's desires will be met. Faith, to paraphrase Martin Luther, is something to be found somewhere beneath the left nipple. (Think about it!)

A common query of the ego is, 'How is my visualisation likely to manifest? It feels as if it ought to be availed of an appropriate set of directions that will lead to its eventual destination. Too much of this probing confers a lack of faith and it ought to be understood that the finite can never be amply aware of the infinite; the limited (conscious) is unable to know of the entirety of the unlimited (unconscious). When the individual cannot have faith in the unseen, the mind is perplexed in its struggle to arrive at a solution of just how the imagined thing will come into existence, simultaneously forgetting about its own limited awareness. This is why we are asked to let go of the reins and have faith, for that map of directions that would plot the route to our envisioned goal does not exist. Nor is there a timetable that charts precisely when our dream is to be realised, and we should abandon all conjecture of the 'how will it happen' problem, forthwith. There is an old saying that a watched pot never boils and applied to the realm of creative imagination it is a most fitting aphorism: when you have visualised for something, let go of it, for whilst you are consciously holding on to it the unconscious does not have it. It is the old law of action-reaction: by continuing to think of your goal after having directed attention to its images in visualisation, it is like preventing it from reaching the unconscious lower levels, and thus dissipating the energy content hitherto generated. Consequently, no reaction in the outer world can take place unless one lets go of the thought.

GOD AND THE PSYCHE

There exists a universal expression of unconscious faith in each human being, though its manner varies from person to person. In astrological symbolism it is represented by the experience of the planet Jupiter, and its placement on the birth chart points to one's subjective contact with the archetype and how one will unconsciously employ it. Without wishing to lapse into astrological discussion, let me just say that Jupiter on one's natal chart symbolises that within us which promotes a faith in the future, the planting of the seeds of possibility in events which lie ahead, behind which exists a sense of meaning in life. When we see this archetype demonstrated, it is in the person who expresses a confident expectation that their slice of life will be duly served up, whose sense of adventure and thirst for living never fails to infect those of a more taciturn, cautious nature. Traditionally, the planet, or rather the human experience of what it symbolises, is indistinguishable from what we are fond of calling good luck, fortune, opportunity, providence. Whereas during the Dark Ages this deity may have been externalised (in the same way that Jesus is today for many Christians), we now understand it to be part of the individual psyche. If then, good fortune depends on an inner component in the subject's psychological make-up, how does the process really assert itself?

It would be helpful to discuss the phenomenon as a full expression of the life of an individual, for inner psyche and outer reality are, in the final analysis, bound together with an invisible cord. The machinations of faith derive from an inner attitude that encourages one's life to run smoothly and the person trapped in the web of routine, clock-watching, or fretting when the bus is late could benefit indeed from letting go this attachment to schedules and over-careful planning. This individual knows full well of the opposite character: the one who seemingly never worries and takes things for granted, which is another way of saying that things are taken on faith, and indeed, the latter finds that what he or she needs *is* granted. Unmindfulness about detail, the arresting of control over mundane matters, not taking direct action or drawing up a detailed strategy, apparently denies the fruits of accomplishment, but this is the same individual who just 'happens' to be offered the job you have been trying to land for the past several months, who somehow runs into the right people at the right time and generally sails through life with relative ease while you end up cast adrift on the rocks of disappointment. Thus it can be seen that a prevailing attitude of *laissez-faire* is instrumental in the creation and perpetuation of harmonious conditions and it is perhaps ironic that it is not the carefully organised person, steadily climbing the ladder of success, upon whom fortune smiles the most, but the individual who takes things for granted.

Such behaviour is bound up with an unconscious process of which the individual is usually unaware, hence not realising why they tend to be more fortunate than average. The faith invested in nature, the expectation that Lady Luck should be secretly waiting around every street corner is so close to them that they never stop to think about it, simply getting on with living and leaving it to her to sort out the rest. Typically, this universal force is projected on to God (and the perversion of it on to Satan) so that the results are interpreted as divine intervention, thus the individual escapes responsibility for even the good things which happen. That God can be found in the unconscious now seems to be quite plausible, especially with the revelations about the psyche afforded by such luminaries as Carl Jung, Alan Watts, Charles Haanel and U.S. Andersen, indeed, Andersen's exhortation to 'let go and let god' points towards one's becoming a vehicle for this energy, and sums up the whole message of this chapter in five simple words.

One often describes something's opposite in order to make clearer, that which one intends to illustrate in the first place, thus unconscious faith can be examined in relation to fear, that uncomfortable thorn in the side which causes the ego to shift so restlessly in its chair. Moreover, fear is just as irrational as is the kind of faith I am discussing — barring the kind of instinctive fear when one is in actual physical danger — and it appears to be far easier for many to succumb to the spectre of doubt than it is to relax in assurance of the inner, creative powers. Fear, if it is entertained for any length of time, becomes a pernicious malady and gives birth to a whole list of horrors so well known that they need not be repeated here. A common epidemic these days is a fear of the future, a state of unknowingness which goads the individual into the need for arranging affairs for tomorrow with painstaking accuracy simply to remain in complete command of the environment, however, this pattern of behaviour proves to be inimical to peace of mind. For when action is based on fear, no matter how much the fear goes unrecognised by the ego, the unconscious must respond accordingly and cast the appropriate spell. One may find this individual attempting to overcompensate for anxieties as they are expressed to others: apparent self-confidence and faith in personal abilities. This is a questionable mask, not merely because it is often transparent to others, but because the inner silent cry becomes more audible as a result since the individual is aggravating the fear in trying to run away from it. At the other end of the spectrum we find the person in whom the fear is made conscious, for example in the apprehensive individual whose finger rests eternally on the panic button, which is all too easily pressed when a crisis occurs and often is pressed unnecessarily, simply because a crisis is expected.

The uncertain tomorrow in all of its ephemerality can, and does, lead the fearful into a dark, hostile labyrinth. The subtle motivation at work here is a human need for security, to know that a certain experience can be repeated again, to know that plans will go to schedule. Consequently the individual often attempts to nail appointments down so securely that he or she believes there is little chance of them ever being broken. But we find ourselves confronted with many situations that we instinctively know we *cannot* control through an act of volition, and either we trust them to work out harmoniously or perpetuate the self-defeating attempt to command what goes on outside of the self. We cannot know for sure who we will meet tomorrow, what will happen to us, whether or not the bus will be late, how we will feel, precisely what our minds will be on, and it is this lack of knowing which breeds the germ of fear, no matter how small. If we cannot be equipped with details of that uncertain tomorrow and be armed for any eventuality, many of us become inwardly restless, and it is this guarded attitude which ensures anxiety for the following day.

So what happens when we relinquish the attempt to subordinate everything to the ego and put faith in tomorrow, handing our plans over to God, or the unconscious? A natural process follows directly on the heels of this submission, since one has created a space allowing the energies a channel through which to express themselves, consequently as the process works itself out, one encounters opportunities related to the intended goal. As one might expect, now is the time to act and make full use of the path that has been cleared, for some interplay between act of will and submission to the inner powers is necessary and it is then left up to the individual to discover how to tread the middle path. Going with the flow does not mean being arbitrarily led through life's many doorways under someone else's direction, open to all that falls into one's path, though this is less of a problem to the human being than its other extreme of battering with the will against unwanted circumstances, resisting the flow because one has already decided on its direction in advance. How many times has one marked out a path of attainment in the external world only to find a closed sign at the end of the road, with accompanying reaction that there is now nowhere else to go? This kind of insular response is dangerous if carried to extremes, and even a little hindsight will reveal the fact that there are many other branch roads leading to the same kind of fulfilment, and the inner promise that there *are* many more such roads to encounter may be guarantee enough of success. Yet the individual is often at pains to discover this inner assurance, and it cannot be acquired by reading the right books either. It can only be discovered via living experience, whereby the individual becomes a living testimony of the laws of nature when thoughts entertained submerge into the unconscious and attract their likeness in events that follow. Expressed another way, think of health, wealth, love or whatever you care to mention, let go of it and it will think *for* you.

ORPHEUS IN THE UNCONSCIOUS

It may appear when viewed from the periphery that in letting go of the thought that it has 'disappeared', that the power has been turned off. Yet the reverse is true, for the thought has not ceased to exist, it has merely slipped from consciousness, found a new breeding ground down below and has assumed an invisible power. For it to exert a creative force in complying with our demands it asks of our faith, our trust, the sanction for it to operate in its own peculiar fashion. This human dilemma is mythologised in the celebrated figure of Orpheus from the Greek tale. According to the tradition, he tries to recover his dead wife Eurydice from the Underworld, the route to which commences with the journey across the river Styx with Charon the ferryman, and continues past the three-headed dog Cerberus, who guards its entrance. Because of Orpheus' intense grief at losing his wife, the underworld god, Hades, consents to let him return to earth with his wife on condition that he *believes* she is following him, that he trusts Hades' word and doesn't look behind him whilst leaving. Unfortunately, his doubt is so overwhelming that he must turn around, only to see Eurydice slip away from him and vanish from sight for ever.

What might this myth be said to symbolise? In relation to faith, it is an enactment of what happens when the conscious ego refuses to trust in a force mightier than its own, for when we do not believe that that power exists, it tends to work behind our backs in all sorts of subversive ways. When all is said and done, the will plays a relatively small part in engineering and manifesting a visualisation, for when the seeds of imagery have been sown, it is left up to the unconscious to arrange knowingly the settings in which one's goal can be realised. Orpheus wanted his wife back, to him, the treasure hard to attain, and if we are to acquire our own riches it is necessary to honour that god abiding in the unconscious, which in everyday terms translates as faith in the creative powers and the willingness to let them work for us. That abiding power in the depths of the mind (in this case, the figure of Hades) will grant our wishes if we attune ourselves to its workings. It is almost as if it says, like Hades, 'I will grant your wish when you have learned to respect me, for it is I who have the *real* power,' and for Orpheus' defiance of the underworld god a hefty price was exacted. The only currency demanded of us is in submission of the ego, for like the tragic hero, our envisioned goal will elude us when we question the creative powers with doubt and scepticism, and that which we might attract through gently giving in — the feminine principle in nature — is repelled further away from us. For Orpheus did not gain access to the Underworld through brute force, he made friends of the dwellers on the threshold with charm and coercion. This same experience is enacted every time the yogi begins a meditation, when the analyst uses active imagination, or the student of tarot allows the images on the cards to speak what words can hardly express.

So many of us embody the doubt of this Greek hero that it is tempting to try and discover what is happening in the uncharted regions for evidence, only to find that 'it' remains tantalisingly out of reach. Had the tragic hero trusted Hades' word he would not have needed to have looked over his shoulder, and would have thus been vindicated with what he was searching for. The face of nature, it would seem, wears a veil that we are forbidden to remove, and if this smacks slightly of romanticism, then consider the number of so-called psychic researchers who investigate the phenomena of other planes of experience only to find that cataloguing laboratory experiments fails to enhance their claims. Whatever it is happening behind our backs, the activities of nature refuse to be seen under the microscope. For this reason it is my opinion that attempts to create an objective science out of what we have termed telepathy, ESP or psychokinesis is like running up a blind alley for the proof lies only in subjective experience. When telepathic communication between two people does occur it happens spontaneously; yet there have been supervised experiments involving two human subjects placed in different rooms, lying prostrate as white noise blares in their ears through headphones while they wait for something to happen.

WHAT'S MOTHER NATURE UP TO?

'Everything in nature contains all the powers of nature. Everything is made of one hidden stuff.' Thus spake Ralph Emerson in one of his majestic essays on the relationship between the human being and the universe. Needless to say, modern day Orpheuses, particularly astronomers, will continue to smile to themselves at the remarks of such thinkers with a kind of patronising, pained superiority, as if they were the words uttered by a four-year-old child who ought to be humoured. Yet sweeping remarks such as the one quoted above, and those of some of the Greek philosophers are, to put not too fine a point on it, verbalised emanations of something felt deep down inside that, indeed, is difficult to convey in an objective fashion, let alone being able to prove it. When Emerson says that everything is made of one hidden stuff, I believe him to be referring to that creative principle of the universe, part of which we embody and make use of with the mind and have christened the Law of Attraction. Our view of reality is more subjective than we care to admit, especially in personal relationships, and objective analysis deludes itself every time it presents a rational and absolute answer to one of nature's mysteries, as a hardy attempt is made to remove that veil.

Here we are back to the land of the subjective, for physics can only venture so far in its objectivity before it stumbles upon the *bête noire* of the scientist, that twilight zone they have called the 'grey area' where unexplainable happenings, like people levitating or the visit of the local poltergeist, draw a predictably incredulous, if not suspicious, attitude. And by its own nature, science is worlds apart from the Church's idea of God and the Creation, yet physics and religious dogma share something in common. Both the erudite professor versed in the nature of atomic structure and the little old lady knocking on the door with this month's magazine bearing the heading 'Does God Want To End The World?', are no nearer to unlocking the secrets of nature than was Plato in the fifth century BC, though this is not intended as a dig at the great man. Rather, it means to say that no one human being may ever gain total access to the mysterious workings of the universe, or God, *as they are in themselves* (i.e. they cannot be objectified) for one's philosophy of life can derive only from the subject. We interpret what we see in a way that suits us, and to paraphrase Carl Jung, one tends to see best what one can best see oneself; perhaps this is what Plato alludes to when he says that, 'Man is the measure of all things.'

If the meaning of this statement is expanded (for he was originally writing about perception and analysis), it can also be taken to refer to the principle of like attracts like, for the quality of a person's life and of that which is encountered can be measured by the source from which it derives, one's self. For the rationalist who has not seen this truth enacted in his or her own life, the experiences of the human kingdom are arbitrary and just happen to come about. The events foisted upon them are considered (if they ever stop to think about them) to be pure chance, either the hand of fortune or misfortune, for it is impossible for them to consider that their own minds are the authors of creation. To many such individuals, mind is a mere concept since it is invisible (unlike the brain) and is rendered nothing more than a giant computer full of accumulated data. Yet science has opened up an old wound in speculations about the supposed non-relationship between thought and the physical world, for quantum physics has shown that matter is influenced by mind beyond a shadow of doubt. In laboratory tests involving sub-atomic particles, results have demonstrated that the behaviour of what was once thought to be objective and predictable varies according to the intentions of whoever is carrying out the test; the objective experiment is affected by the expectations of the subject who is performing it. This conclusion drawn from quantum physics ought to rip apart many of the prejudices of those who insist that the mind has no power to influence the physical world, and as one of its pioneers, Niels Bohr, points out; 'Anyone who is not shocked by the quantum theory has not understood it.'

Such discoveries as these mean that the universe is more complex than we can readily appreciate, and I recall one of those investigative TV specials that attempt to unravel the enigma surrounding subjects like telepathy and psychokinesis in a 'Tomorrow's World' type format. The programme was a veiled attempt to pass off metaphysical happenings as red herrings that appeal to the innate human curiosity, and to expose people who claimed to have had such experiences as hoaxers. But I laughed when the presenter asked, in all reverence, a question to the effect of, 'What kind of universe is it that hides its secrets from the prying eyes of objective science?' Indeed.

Yet one of the secrets that nature does let us in on, is that the human being is his or her own creator and the circumstances surrounding any human being are reflections of this general consciousness, and if one looks closely enough the fact can be seen distinctly. The maxim will not appeal to the 'well prove it then' brigade because the evidence cannot be laid down on the table for inspection like so many exhibit As in a court-room trial. That each individual unwittingly operates the Law of Attraction is unprovable in those terms or criteria which the scientist would require. Imagine the futility of trying to prove that visualisation works: this would require a lengthy experiment involving weekly, more likely monthly reports to the monitor. Theoretically, when the envisioned goal has finally been realised, one would be able to report that the experiment had been a success, until one realises that to a rationalist one's proof would count as no proof at all, for it is likely to be regarded as mere chance. Furthermore, in visualisation one would not normally broadcast one's desire since this has the unfortunate side-effect of dissipating its energies or attracting the counteracting thoughts of others. Making sincere attempts to convince the sceptic of the reality of astral energies is like spitting into an oncoming breeze — it keeps blowing back into your face.

I am reminded of a former acquaintance of mine who thoroughly rejects matters concerned with the psyche, especially astrology, which he refers to as 'that horoscope tripe', though this is complimentary when compared with other epithets I have heard for it. He has chosen to believe in the non-existence of this realm and so his surroundings mirror the pattern of his thoughts: nothing ever out of the ordinary happens to him; his whole existence comprises of a well-ordered routine, careful and safe, filled with sensible, reasonable, level-headed people, yet every so often nature (apparently) plays a trick on him and he encounters something which he is at a loss to understand. Colleagues at work inexplicably lose their tempers with him, he comes into contact with irrational types or those of a more primitive (his word, not mine) nature, but the most damning evidence that here was a mortal who was employing his inner mind as a destructive force was when his wife unexpectedly walked out on him, never to return. If in this case we have a thoroughly reasonable and placid-natured individual who exudes peaceful temperament and rarely speaks ill of anyone, then why is the foundation of his life mercilessly pulled from underneath him by the hand of fate? Is the Law of Attraction flawed and unpredictable in its operations?

The empirical truth remains, and in fact there is no contradiction, though on the face of it is a paradox, that not only does like attract but opposites too (and there are further illustrations of this in the next chapter). This often leads the individual to feel thwarted because he or she runs into something that was not expected, something alien and often hostile that yet again produces the anguished cry, 'Why me?'. The desertion of my friend's wife did not appear at face value to be the right thing to occur, but it spoke volumes about what was brewing in the unconscious, about what he was inwardly refusing to become aware of, either through semi-ignorance or the resistance of the ego. True enough, this was indeed a peaceable and thoroughly reasonable guy, but with this kind of strictly logical way of assimilating experience he could not detect the finer currents flowing around him, or rather he preferred to ignore them. For no one is so insensitive to atmosphere that they cannot perceive unrest brewing, and he admitted as much when he remarked that something was not quite right. In fact, he had brought about the end of his marriage himself by setting in motion a train of events he could not eradicate by smoothing over them, and it was with some misgivings that he consented to have his astrological birth chart set up and analysed.

The chart, as I had expected, fittingly portrayed symbols of the kind of attitude with which he would approach the world, and what, in reply, the world would play back to him. It was only later when I discovered his underlying resentment of his wife's two young children, for this had been her second marriage, that it became clear how he had poisoned his unconscious with the hostility and anger he refused to express consciously. He secretly despised having to cope with the added responsibility of shopping, babysitting, buying toys and suffering the noise of two healthy youngsters, yet consciously, he had tried to accept the situation and adapt to what was expected of him, a role that he wore as uncomfortably as a badly fitting suit. Thus did the garment become too tight to wear easily, and he began to shirk some of his duties by forgetting to carry out certain tasks, spending money on the wrong items or arranging to be unavailable for babysitting. He had built up a considerable amount of unconscious resentment against these little requirements, for so long considered superfluous, which revealed itself, though cleverly camouflaged, in the petty rebellions mentioned above — as the old saying goes, 'If it don't come out in the wash, it come out in the rinse.' His unconscious correctly interpreted these little acts of defiance as his inner desire to be rid of the straitjacket of limitation, and since he avoided a direct confrontation, the resistances accumulated inwardly and formed the substance of what he *really* felt about the situation. Unconsciously, he rejected it, or rather he genuinely only accepted the woman he lived with. If he had known that his inner psyche would respond and act on his orders he would have stopped in his tracks to examine the motives for his actions. That which he refused to become acquainted with, namely his distaste at being father to someone else's children, settled into the inner recesses of his mind and was eventually performed as an event in his life, for that is in the nature of the beast.

Deep within, my friend wanted no association with this aspect of domestic life, so it was removed from him. The Lord giveth and the Lord taketh away. When he first consulted me, he could not appreciate that his negative thoughts about looking after his wife's children, which leaked out in his behaviour, could cut any deeper than would a mild dissatisfaction, notwithstanding acting as a subversive force that would engineer the destruction of the whole situation; without realising it he was actively signing his own death warrant. In the end, he got what he asked for, he was relieved of the burden of his invidious duties, at the expense of seeing his wife walk out of his life forever. The maxim that opposites attract was enacted in this particular instance, the opposites, one could say, were psychological energies of which he chose to remain ignorant, for he never actually used the words 'resentment' or 'distaste', though his actions spoke for themselves, and he was sufficiently aware of feeling trapped in this environment. These qualities existed for him unconsciously and the buried hostility found its way into the external, culminating in his wife's desertion. Usually, when one speaks of like attracting like one is referring to similar qualities that are encountered in either a person or situation, but opposites attract also since attributes of which one is unconscious draw to themselves their likeness in individuals who make use of them consciously, or as in my friend's case, in fated events that act out the inner dramas for them.

CHAPTER 4
CREATION IN MIND — THE POWERHOUSE BELOW

Emanations from the mind travel like faithful planets in their measured orbit, and like those heavenly bodies, thoughts will return to the place from which they first departed.

Certain signs precede certain events.
Cicero

In order to be 'careful of what we want because we just might get it', it is necessary to take a closer look at how we employ the conscious mind and make an attempt to lift the veil on what lies beneath, since it is possible to see how the unconscious does its bidding for us. Its effect is observable by the very conditions we experience in life, as things do not happen to us, we cause them to happen, and this strikingly simple message will ring out a chord in those perceptive individuals who have already realised this truth. The main purpose then in this chapter, is to show how one's unconscious responses to life determine what will be accumulated down there and will thus proceed to design one's particular fate, since whatever is taken in and made real soon becomes a definite, concrete reality. Upon this maxim is visualisation based, hence, mental images are something more than the chimerical fruits of, say, Lear, Blake or Picasso; they are something which possess a tangible substance, although how tangible is open to consideration. One can find various examples of the tangibility of mind or thought energy in the sensitive individual who is able to perceive atmosphere on entering a room, or is able to know what someone is feeling simply by virtue of the other's presence. I was once intrigued by a friend who is a tarot reader when he asked in a warm, phlegmatic tone, 'Would you like to talk about whatever it is that's worrying you?' Not having broadcast any signals whatsoever as to what was going on inside and feeling quite satisfied that it was well hidden, his remark came almost as an invasion of the soul. How could he know what I was feeling? It is this mysterious process of perception that once and for all demonstrates that something emanates from the individual perhaps in the form of vibration, a something which cannot be detected with the normal five senses, yet exists nonetheless.

The life of the mind is a constantly shifting event, always happening, a random ceaseless flow of thoughts which suddenly impinge upon our consciousness, yet why it operates in this fashion we do not know. One's unconscious content is formed by the reaction to the objective (the outside world, other people) and subjective (memories, impressions, fleeting thoughts) and this response can either be subliminal or fully conscious, moreover it does not matter as to whether or not the information we digest is true, it is the tone of the reaction that counts. For this is the stage in the process that determines what we will create for ourselves both as a personality and in terms of environmental conditions, as our impressions form what we believe to be true about ourselves and the world and hence they form the base from which we operate. Any action, trivial or meaningful, impresses the unconscious with certain information about what one believes to be true (since one is acting in that way) and here the subtleties take over, for the unconscious does not argue or analyse rationally and brings about conditions in accordance with that belief. As I have pointed out, the determining factor, as far as the creative aspect of mind is concerned, is not whether the belief we have swallowed is accurate, it is the fact that we have swallowed it at all, which in turn draws on certain expectancies about life in general. And indeed, so much of life is determined by our expectations of it: what we expect to hear, what we expect to see, what we expect to feel, most of it accepted on faith.

I once found myself in conversation with a somewhat benign but vacant looking gentleman in the confines of a spiritualist church, and one of his remarks suggested to me that he may have had strong religious leanings. That utterance was: ' . . . whatever it is you accept about life, the Lord will bring it into existence.' His use of the word 'Lord' immediately labelled him, to me, as a 'bible reader', or one of those souls who are fervently convinced that Jesus (the man) is present in their lives, until I learned that he was a white magician who had studied Crowley and W. B. Yeats. Those two words of his, 'accept' and 'Lord', can be translated into psychological parlance thus: accepting is the taking on faith of a particular idea, the belief that something will come to pass, and if one understands the Lord to be that enigmatic, creative power in the unconscious, then the dictum is seen to be empirically valid, since it has been borne out by experience many times over. The power invested in this hinterland relies for its source on the person at the gateway between inner and outer life (the ego) as the individual must decide what will be accepted down there, which is why blind faith, illogical though it may be, works wonders for the visualiser.

The phenomenon whereby 'the Lord will bring into existence', whatever the individual has formulated as part of their mental make-up, is curious only to the mind that is too ready to pass off external happenings as coincidence, chance or miracle, though it stands as a thoroughly natural and unsensational fact of life. The consequences of human cause and effect are readily seen in the light of psychological energies (not to be confused with psychic energy, which is the ultimate source of all one's energies). It is this approach that I now wish to adopt in order to describe the inner dynamics of visualisation and mental creation. However, I

70

will not be discussing thought forms, mental vibrations or the astral planes; my intention is to present an interpretation that embraces both scientific (in the sense that it is based on quantifiable experience) and symbolic approaches, since there is a world existing out of reach of the normal senses that is not directly knowable, yet can be demonstrated by the use of allegory.

Analytical psychology has uncovered the effects of unconscious energy through observing the experiences of subjects who are out of touch with themselves, that is, unaware of the unconscious nature of mind. Psychological energies of which we are unaware have a knack of finding their way into outer experience, either in ailments of the body, one-to-one relationships, or the fate of the individual. Both astrology and its infant brother depth psychology, have demonstrated the phenomenon called 'projection', whereby one's unconscious content is projected on to others, usually wherever there is a strong emotional reaction, though this need not always be the case. It is exemplified admirably in personal relationships where whatever is unconscious in one partner will be projected on to, and expressed by the other.

What then exactly, is meant by unconscious content? It is common to build up a general picture of ourselves to form the self-image of the ego, which is expressed as a conscious personality; the ways in which we think, act and tend to feel, but as each mortal cannot be everything at once, some negative qualities go downstairs and become part of the unconscious scenery. To take a common archetype, there is the shy, self-effacing person who is consciously aware of being generous to his family, hardworking, modest, thoroughly loyal to his mates and helpful towards little old ladies. These are the qualities he values about himself and has impressed on to the ego, and no-one around him might ever stop to consider that there was anything 'lacking' in him, but depth psychology would say otherwise. What is in fact lacking in him is the expression of qualities opposed to those of his conscious nature, and though this need not cause him any serious problems, it does mean that he will find them in involvements with other people. There is the aggressive shop-floor engineer who has to put up with the office wimp, the benevolent Samaritan who feels tried by the tightfistedness of the miser, the heady intellectual Eton graduate who cannot comprehend the sentimentality of his dog-loving friend. And so on. If like attracts like was the prevailing and ultimate truth, then these apparently conflicting opposites would never find one another, so we find that our shy, nice-guy model above finds qualities in his wife that are at times difficult to deal with. The natural pull of opposites may mean that his wife exudes qualities in direct contrast to his generally taciturn nature: an energetic, self-assertive personality, the urge to dominate, pure self-ishness, laziness, etc. To the objective eye, the partnership may resemble the classic mismatch, yet there is nothing the individual will attract from the outside that is not already contained within his psyche, which is precisely why he has attracted such a woman in the first place — the qualities consciously expressed in *her* are part of his unformed, un-lived, unconscious content.

To the analytical mind the unconscious is a strange beast, for it contains paradoxes that cannot be resolved: if the unconscious partakes of qualities in contrast to those of our ego expression, playing the proverbial devil's advocate, then it cannot at the same time create for us whatever we have consciously taken on faith through the acceptance of the ego. Expressed simply, it cannot oppose us and move with us simultaneously, yet this is how it often appears to operate, but I believe this to be nothing more than that, an appearance. The idea is made clearer if one considers different levels of unconsciousness. If one takes the conscious mind (that of which we are aware and readily express) as a reference point, one can appreciate levels of awareness that function just beneath the surface (memory and feelings which are readily recalled, unconscious operation of bodily organs) and it is this area which collects our impressions from everyday experience. One might say that this represents the knowable, personal part of the unconscious since it is the repository of our gathered experience, but as one moves further away from this area one discovers terrain which appears alien to our everyday awareness. In short, it becomes less personal and unfamiliar, full of qualities which we never even knew we possessed, and in a sense don't possess because they are unconscious, so we meet them in projections. Then even further away it comprises of those mysterious elements that intrude upon our normal, wake-up-and-smell-the-coffee existence. Anyone who has undergone intense transformations in their life during which they must live out irrational compulsions, uncharacteristically obsessive behaviour, feelings of other-wordly ecstasy, for example falling in love, or the sudden, compelling desire for drastic change, have unearthed some of this deep unconscious layer of themselves. And I mention all of this for I believe that mid-ground of the unconscious, where lies our unknown potential, to be the penultimate creator that brings about those situations we have longed for in visualisation when that energy is projected.

Projection is the way in which unconscious energy finds a way out as it reproduces its likeness in an appropriate physical object, the purpose being to seek consciousness. The observations of projections between husband and wife, mother and son, boss and employee, as recounted on the analyst's couch, attest to this maxim. Thus, our mental images are the foundations for layers of energy which become stored in the unconscious, and as we have seen with projection, are working towards self-expression in the daily life of an individual through something we call attraction, action/reaction, and sometimes fate. But what about those little brick walls we occasionally run into, those awkward quirks of fate over which we have no control? The person who is aware (or 'hip', to use an adjective from sixties' hippy culture) is able to see that the particular outcomes in his or her daily life are the consequences of forces the individual has set in motion, the logical result of a certain interaction of psychological energies. But most of us are entirely unconscious of these fundamental aspects of our being and they draw us into situations that assume the mask of an ugly, irrevocable fate. American astrologer Robert Hand, in his remarkable *Planets in Transit*, writes about this experience as 'what you unconsciously programme your environment to do', which is contingent upon one's general *modus operandi*; that is, not merely ways of behaving, means of thinking and acting, etc., but *why* we behave and act like that, *why* we hold certain attitudes. The 'why' we are often entirely unaware of, the unconscious knows about and instructs the universe to respond to our actions.

ONCE UPON A TIME

So far we have discussed the likely emergent effects, through projection, of inner energies which are no different in kind from those produced by visualisation. Now comes 'story time', an enchanting tale beloved of the under fives who are read to in bed before lights out at 7:30, only this time with a difference, for what follows is a psychological interpretation of *The Elves And the Shoemaker*. To begin with, the process whereby a visualisation becomes a reality corresponds to the way in which the artist, poet, author, or musician eventually brings forth a creation. The lyricist, for instance, may have to sort through a jigsaw puzzle of disconnected words and couplets before he or she can reproduce the original idea in an acceptable form. Whilst attempting to lay down intended ideas on paper, the artist may even give up halfway, either abandoning the task completely or leaving it until later. Now the unconscious goes to work (this being the 'upper region' of the unconscious which was discussed earlier) arranging the finished article without conscious direction, and in an unguarded moment the lyricist will 'have' it: the completed work will flow through as pen is put to paper. The unconscious knew what was being looked for, and provided the most adequate means of accomplishment, depending on the material given to it. This working relationship between the two aspects of mind can be glimpsed in the aforementioned children's story with the Shoemaker and the Elves as caricatured elements of the psyche, and when mental images are the material handed to the unconscious, the stuff is worked upon by those handy elves until the end-product can appear in the flesh, as it were.

Myth and fairy tale provide a useful symbolic language for the unfoldment of unconscious activity. 'Elves' allegorises the interaction between conscious (visualisation) and unconscious (creation) during the process of making image into flesh. In this particular tale, a somewhat poverty stricken and elderly shoemaker who lives with his spouse has just finished the laborious task of cutting out the leather from which he will later fashion a brand new pair of shoes. But it is late, and having decided to retire for the night, he leaves the unfinished material on his worktop ready to set to work the next day. To his astonishment, when he comes down the next morning, there stands on the table a finished, beautifully crafted pair of shoes. They are so perfect that he is quickly able to sell them and acquire more material to work with. Needless to say there are other elements to this story, but it is this part of the narrative which concerns us here.

The patterning of the idealised article is all that is required, no interference is necessary. This is symbolised in the work of cutting out the requisite shapes of leather and then leaving them to be finished, though, of course, the Shoemaker did not know he was leaving it to someone else. Similarly, the conscious ego is often unaware of the extent to which the unconscious can exercise a force that brings about a change in one's conditions, or indeed of its ability to take over from where the individual will left off, and finish the task. Nevertheless, after having witnessed the finished article (in this case a pair of shoes) the old man is understandably curious, and after he has laid out his patterns in the usual manner, he hides and waits in the darkened silence to see what will happen. Then, four or five tiny elves appear and proceed to set to work on the leather shapes left by the shoemaker, with which they eventually craft another magnificent pair of footwear. The Shoemaker looks on in silent amazement, not wishing that they should be disturbed, overjoyed that they should be performing such splendid work for him. The elves are symbolic of unconscious forces, or little helpers, that are activated when the conscious mind is struggling towards the realisation of a given goal; they are the creative elements in the old man's unconscious that vindicate his instinctive faith in them. Consequently, when he arises the following day he finds that the work is done. He does not question their power, their workmanship, their ability to shoulder such a sophisticated piece of work, he simply allows them to get on with it, like so many managing directors who leave the responsibilities of the office to their efficient secretaries.

There is no fixed pattern to which the unfoldment of envisioned goals must conform. On the one hand, the result may come all at once, out of the blue, and on the other may announce its impending arrival by a series of coincidences. In these cases it is as if certain instances of good luck serve as an omen that the transformation is in progress, that whatever it is that is apparently happening, has begun for sure; the unexpected phone call, the advertisement in a newspaper that catches the eye, the unpredicted encounter with a friend who imparts certain information. These unconscious arrangements disguised as random happenings are the handiwork of forces set in motion during the imaging ritual, the fashioning of inchoate material gradually taking shape. The potter takes his block of clay, throws it on the wheel, and slowly a recognisable form starts to emerge, evolving into a shape with which one might identify until before us stands the finished object. And so it is with manifestations of inner images, but what has happened to bring the results to you?

Viewed from the surface, it would seem that the external universe undergoes a process of change that will finally usher in the desired conditions, and this nascent stage of development can only be seen in retrospect. Thus when the sought-after goal is realised, one may look back to the occurrences arbitrarily taking their place in the scheme of events leading up to the final result. For instance, suppose I envisage myself in a new job, perhaps as the supervisor of a large office building. I would visualise my journey to work, the scene in my office on arriving, my secretary making tea, and feel the satisfaction of having achieved such a position of authority, especially when I inspect my wage slip (all this is bearing in mind that I am actually experienced or capable enough of carrying out such a role). Somewhere out there, as a result of my visualisation, events of which I have no direct knowledge will finally culminate to the point whereby the position which I visualised becomes a real possibility. One admonition however: never visualise to compete, i.e. never imagine yourself stepping into the shoes of someone already known to you, for you would be intruding upon the path of another individual, an act which may rightly be termed black magic. If you usurp the position of some actual person, which they have attracted as a result of their own thought patterns, then expect one day that the illegitimate place you have just stolen will be removed from you by the same forces which have hitherto worked in your favour. If you must use this power for devilish pursuits, see a psychiatrist.

To press on with the example, let us say that after two months visualising my new working environment, I learn from the grapevine that a similar type of position is being advertised on the current job market. At the material level, any number of events may have worked themselves out to clear the way for my opportunity to arise: someone at that organisation could have retired, been dismissed, moved to another area or maybe the company has taken on more work and they need the extra staff. Whatever the case, the unconscious has attracted the appropriate conditions, and various shiftings around have taken place in order for the visualisation to work; you will find this to have happened in virtually all cases of such an attraction, however indirect you may feel your influence has been. Other individuals will necessarily unconsciously contribute to this subtle game, as elements of the environment change places to reveal the way in; such conditions appear to be happening outside of the visualiser until the goal is reached and the connection can be seen. The subsequent real-life story exemplifies this principle of how the unconscious directs one to the intended goal when outer conditions have been satisfied, since inner energies will attempt to find the most appropriate physical outlet.

LOUISE'S STORY

Once upon a time there lived a rather shy and lonely girl of twenty years, who had recently begun to feel a little cut off from the mainstream of human contact. She was perceptive enough to acknowledge that these inner stirrings were born out of her fundamental need to relate intimately to someone of the opposite sex, especially on an emotional level. (For the purposes of readers learned in astrology, the subject of this tale is a Sun/Moon Scorpio, Venus in Virgo and Mars in Scorpio.) She had already come to a realisation of the energies living within her and sought to learn more of these drives through literature on psychology and the occult, which in turn led her to discover the principles governing visualisation. Fittingly enough, she decided to employ the technique to attract someone with whom she could share the wealth of feeling which needed to be expressed; that she had discovered the presence of envy at witnessing the shared affection of others was evidence enough (to her) that she was missing out on something.

Louise began in earnest with the requisite techniques, at first finding difficulty in retaining mental images for more than a few minutes though she was determined to succeed with the practice. As is peculiar to the nature of the law of attraction, she stumbled upon other material expounding the virtues of creative visualisation and thus grew her appreciation of unconscious mechanisms and the labyrinthine world of the inner mind. I ought to point out at this stage that at the onset of the imaging period, Louise had actually set down a date on which she anticipated meeting this new suitor, notwithstanding his idealised personal qualities which she had animated with the characteristics of a particular sign of the zodiac (Taurus, incidentally). Archetypal expressions of earthy common sense, a quiet warmth and a strong physical nature represented, to her, some of the ideal traits to be found in the man whom she would encounter on that date she had scribbled down with 'some vague notion of meeting someone at the party'. The party referred to was the celebration of her twenty-first birthday, for which a function room had duly been hired.

With the passing of approximately one month she made the classic error of expecting too much too soon, with the spectre of doubt threatening to occupy a permanent place in her conscious mind, except when she would sit wondering if the stranger sat opposite on the bus, or at the next table in a coffee bar, or the guy waiting in the adjoining room at her music lesson might be 'him'. Understandably, this attitude provoked considerable frustration as she began to wonder if visualisation worked at all, for being a neophyte visualiser and knowing full well that not everyone is blessed with an earth-moving Mills and Boon romance, her logic began to get the upper hand. This not unnatural state of affairs is what hampers the progress of many enthusiastic persons who try visualising for the first time: they look around themselves and to their chagrin, discover that nothing has changed, although this is only an appearance. Change *has* occurred, on the inner level, and there exists an explanation common to scholars of the occult that may soothe the restless minds of those visualisers who feel that the results are too slow in arriving, or indeed that their efforts have been in vain because no evidence exists on the material plane to suggest that their image-work has taken effect. The explanation concerns itself with the idea of separate planes of existence, or experience, and their different rates of vibration. The wise adept may speak of 'thought forms descending the planes', that when first conceived appear on the mental plane before its journey through the astral and etheric regions until they finally descend to the plane of matter. This concept, though abstruse, is made clearer when one considers thought as a thing, an entity, which takes on an emotional content and imbues itself with a kind of little personality, which in turn attracts a material entity composed of a similar substance. It is only muddled when one thinks in terms of spatial layers with the mental plane the top of the scale and the material at the bottom.

Louise had learned of this occult teaching and relaxed in the knowledge that patience would prove to be her greatest friend at this time of un-knowing, yet she continued to check the calendar and it *was* getting uncomfortably close to the date she had written down, so she felt suspended between a vague scepticism and the almost holy belief that her wish would be granted. About three days before her birthday, *en route* home from her piano lesson on a freezing, wintry night, she was sitting having a drink with a friend in one of the many public houses of her home town. She had a folder of sheet music opened up on the bar, attempting to explain to her friend Clare the difference between treble and bass clef. Here is where Madame Destiny showed her hand, for the whole situation had been an unconscious set-up in order to direct our heroine to her goal. Whilst the two girls were discussing the merits of Bach and Schubert and who else Louise ought to add to the still meagre invitation list for the party, the barman approached and, in mock aggressive tones, told them not to litter up his bar with paper. After he had asked them what they were doing, introduced himself, and conducted a lengthy account on the six-stringed virtuoso delights of Bert Weedon, he bought drinks for the girls and continued with the conversation whilst serving the odd customer. It was at this point that Clare suggested, in all seriousness, that Louise might invite this eccentric man to her party, and immediately she surprised herself by replying, 'Why not?'

The plot now becomes a little thicker, for even though Louise knew that this was not the man she was waiting for, owing to the fact that he was over forty and married, she had unwittingly participated in bringing about the realisation of her desire. The barman was duly invited and accepted, adding that he would if permissible, bring along his wife, then, after a long pause, he enquired as to whether the birthday girl was married. When told that she was not, he announced that a nephew of his, who was presently single and had just moved into his own house, would probably love to attend also, 'if you'd like to meet him, that is'. On the heels of this revelation came the third degree from Louise on the height, hair colour, age, facial characteristics and personality of this mystery man who just might correspond to her visualisation, at least in terms of personal qualities. Arrangements were made to meet said barman, together with wife and nephew, at the designated venue on the date Louise had recklessly scribbled on a note pad — November 1st, 1980. Needless to say the envisioned relationship began from that meeting; it *had* to happen, for she had already decided upon it in her imagination long before. And they both, hopefully, lived happily ever after. (Incidentally, her partner's birthday is in May, when the Sun is in Taurus.)

A few issues could be raised here, in relation to the seemingly minor incident which acted as a catalyst for a considerably larger one: what if the two girls had walked into a different pub? What if they had avoided the mildly impertinent barman? Why was Louise's friend suddenly struck with the idea of inviting him to the party? And whatever possessed Louise to agree to it? For with hindsight, one can see these are the pieces that fell into place all too easily, certainly with no deliberate action on Louise's part, before the jigsaw was complete, even that particular drinking establishment had been suggested by Clare. From the psychological standpoint, she had been unconsciously drawn to that situation and the other two individuals were merely acting out their apportioned roles in Louise's play, the one she had staged with the assistance of the inner creator. Her unconscious knew the route towards the desired destination and guided her with an unseen hand, having first located the appropriate conditions for her plan to come to fruition. Perhaps the questions above are irrelevant, for it simply happened as it did, surely a most convincing piece of evidence that it was the work of the unconscious.

CHAPTER 5

FROM VISUALISATION TO MATERIALISATION

In quiet reflective passivity, unencumbered by the shuffling feet of unwelcome thought, one can see the whole future at a glance. Only in this meditative state can one rouse the inner creator, for whilst the mind that looks outwards is full of meaningless words and voices, the one that looks within can never make itself heard.

'But that's stupid', my friend declared, 'I mean, it doesn't actually *do* anything, it's just pretending.'

'Precisely', came my reply, 'it *sounds* stupid, but it works.' I was discussing the merits of visualisation with a friend who, having long ago acknowledged its powers, could not digest the idea of having the desired object already. That is, behaving as if one were already in possession of the thing visualised for, which calls forth the emotional life of the individual, a guiding hand in bringing desires into reality, for that is where the real source of power lies. True enough, thought is creative, but backed by powerful emotion it acquires a terrific energy and sets the wheels of life force turning. The word 'E-motion' means energy in motion. Thus, if one goes ahead and engages in this plastic experience, invoking the current of emotions that one might normally feel, had one already obtained the desired goal, the experience would be effective in bringing the actual object nearer to us for as we have seen, the unconscious understands the language of feelings very well indeed. Furthermore, psychology has arrived at the conclusion that the central nervous system is unable to discern between matter-of-fact experience and that which is vividly imagined. Both the actual and the synthetic experience are received uninterpreted by the unconscious since it does not have the capacity for rational judgement, hence, to the unconscious, they will both feel the same. For the more your emotions tell you that you 'have' something, the quicker will you have it in the flesh.

The 'As If' technique, pioneered by American psychologist/philosopher William James, makes a suitable companion to the visualising rituals you will be performing later. The emotional response communicates to the unconscious that 'this might be so', that the dream is real, and this creates energies within the psyche that act like a magnet ready to bring forth the corresponding material object. In practice, it is necessary to create a mental blueprint and furnish it with the requisite props engendering a true child-like imagination — if you can stand it. For the barrier you will have to straddle is the interference of the objective mind, the evidence of the physical world reminding you of the irrationality, like some imposing, unwelcome guest. But as we have seen, the unconscious does not speak in the same language, it speaks the language of dreams and intuitions, so it is safe to assume that if it is real enough to your emotions, it will be real enough to the unconscious.

In deploying this technique in order to create a suitable ambience around you, you might for instance, carry around certain material possessions, visit particular locations to spark off the right feelings, jot down various concocted memos (which you will notice quite often) or even wear a particular kind of clothing in order to impress the unconscious that your goal has been reached and it is a living reality. Playing this subtle trick on the inner mind will be effective only so long as your responses are clothed in emotion, and of course, the same holds true for your ritualised imaging. However in the latter case, there ought to be no conflict aroused by the intervention of the rational processes as the ritual should be performed in a semi-meditative state.

THE FIVE COMMANDMENTS

1. Thou Shalt Have Utter Silence To Begin With

2. Thou Shalt Create A Living Image

3. Thou Shalt Dedicate Your Whole Heart To It

4. Thou Shalt Use The 'As If' Technique

5. Thou Shalt Have Faith In The End Result.

Let me just apologise for perhaps sounding like an instruction manual for we have now reached the point of actual practice, the setting up of a ritual, in an undisturbed place, which will enable you to project your visions upon the universe, that great invisible ocean of mind. The first requirement is to slow down the meandering stream of consciousness flowing through the mind, conversations you had earlier, images of places you have just visited, fleeting emotional impressions, etc. Picture to yourself, one of those perspex bubble ornaments filled with clear liquid that when shaken, sends scores of tiny white crystals swirling around the interior until they finally come to rest. When the mind is cluttered with unnecessary distractions it is difficult to maintain a strong visualisation, so the contents must be allowed to settle, like the crystals in the bubble, in order to make room for the images with which you are going to work. Having found a relaxed position, these unwelcome intruders must be prevented from invading your space, through a process of gently yielding and letting the mind quiesce. Those who persist in this discipline will acknowledge that two objects cannot occupy (in the mind) the same space at any one time. Those accomplished in meditation will have experienced the bliss-like effect when thinking has ceased, that is, thinking about something in contrast to the energy of thought itself and indeed, one may suspect that when this takes place the result would be emptiness, a vacuum. The reverse is true: a clearer, purer consciousness arises, for there is no such thing as a void in the mind.

If you can master the art of doing nothing mentally for about ten minutes, the little paradox being that there is really no effort required, for one does not actively try to relax, then you will gain greater access to the inner energies and focus upon the desired images with much greater clarity. Even though the practice of visualisation may aptly be called a ritual, there is no need for the use of magical paraphernalia such as altar cloths, incenses, talismanic charms, anointed candles, although the latter are especially effective. However, the ageless food of love, music, is a great enhancement to the already animated world of inner images for the settings become richer and infused with meaning. Previously, I have myself tuned in easily to the euphonious strains of *Tubular Bells*, some of Pink Floyd's *Dark Side Of The Moon* and *Wish You Were Here* and the magnificent *In The Land of Grey and Pink* by Caravan. Of course it is entirely subjective and a matter of personal taste, so select a piece that evokes meaningful images for you, bearing in mind that the purpose is not to create a lingering distraction where you are carried away by it. It is more along the lines of a guided tour, with you as the guide. In the manipulation of these images whilst bringing out as much life in them as you can, the music serves as a background soundtrack, an incidental mood, whilst your visions play their parts as the leading cast. If it is your baptism at visualising, don't be surprised to find that the images soon begin to lack detail and clarity or tend to dissipate al-together; your conscious image-making faculty has only just been awakened and your ability to retain clear, strong pictures grows in proportion to the amount of effort that is expended, and the practice can be made easier with suitable background music.

Whether you are using the technique in order to attract from the outside (material objects, improved circumstances, another person) or to work upon oneself (greater self-confidence, increased physical energy, weight loss), the rules are the same and failure to comply with them incurs the usual penalties: either the individual succeeds in attracting nothing at all, or becomes co-partner in the invocation of forces above and beyond their ultimate control. In the latter case I refer mainly to visualisations comprising of actual people that are known to you with the emphasis on attracting them for what we are fond of calling 'love and romance' and in the author's opinion, drawing some real person to you so that you can 'have' a relationship is voodoo or black magic, sugar-coated with sentiment and flowers. The visualisation will work, but the results are dependent upon the circumstances surrounding the other person both psychological and material, and indeed, whether or not he or she wants to be attracted in the first place — whatever the case, you will soon find out. By all means, if it is your heartfelt belief that a relationship with person X would work and the present situation does not appear to deny the possibility of it coming to fruition then go ahead and visualise, but bear in mind that the result may also be a focus for unfulfilled expectations and unrequited love. To safeguard against getting your fingers burned, I suggest that you employ your own idealised picture of a partner, which we all have ingrained in the unconscious, and work at making yourself more conscious of the image, for this inner archetype is a representative of your emotional aspirations towards love and romance and the result will be a truer reflection of your real needs. (There is more on this technique in the subsequent chapter.)

One particular law, which American occultist Ophiel describes as the 'sphere of availability', is that one only visualises for something that is going to be within reach. This is simple common sense as one would not hold out one's hand for something that is never likely to exist, yet the temptation to dream big is so great in some people that they are carried away by the notion that literally anything is possible. However, depending on the envisioned goal, the novice visualiser may indeed realise a dream (for instance, a large house in the country, the managing directorship of a large business concern, a huge pools win) only to discover later that they cannot cope with the reality of it all because of the consequent responsibilities not bargained for. This Frankenstein's monster effect is prevalent among the many people who have been made miserable by the very thing they so ardently sought, or rather, the by-product of that goal-worldly success. Consider the film actors and actresses, pop stars, footballers, and inheritors of huge sums of money whose lives have been irrevocably changed through success that they cannot deal with. In many instances the star attains the fantastic wealth, the fame, the adulation, only to find that nature compensates with the broken marriage, the identity crisis, a hollow emptiness and the desire to return to normal living. If you would put yourself in the same shoes as the sorcerer's apprentice, ensure that you are prepared for big visualisations and that you can handle the realities that come with the dream before ever taking up the wand.

The next rule that must be satisfied is that of filling in as many details as one can muster, for there must be clarity: your visualisation resembles a painting-by-numbers board where each separate strand of colour acts as a detail that will form the finished picture. Paint in as much detail as you can. Let us suppose that your envisioned goal is a larger, brighter, presumably more expensive place in which you will live. Imagine the view from the sumptuous living room, the carefully tended lawn, rose bushes, poplar trees and red brick garden wall, as you recline on your velvet sofa. Take in the contents of surroundings: the cream coloured carpet with matching flock wallpaper, the genuine coal fire, Moroccan tapestried cushions, a Salvador Dali hanging above the fireplace, the nouveau riche onyx ashtray and cigarette lighter. The examples given here are representative of the detail one must include in order to make it real, although the images are only half of this reality. The more sharp and exact are they, the more correct will your results appear at the physical level. With acquired experience it will be possible to feel your way into the images as if they were actually there. Practise touching the objects in your visualised living room, feel the sensation of your velvet settee, handle the cushions at your side, run your fingers along the arms of the furniture. This touching technique adds the element of sensation to your imaging practices and is not merely limited to touch: experiment with the other senses of smell, taste and hearing, the pungent aroma of your tomato plants in the window, the sweet, rather unsubtle sensations of strong, black coffee on your taste buds as you become aware of the intermittent crackling noise of that roaring coal fire. Or something like that.

LIVING IMAGES

So important is the next rule that I have already outlined it previously, and will repeat it here. The visualiser must necessarily participate via feeling whenever conducting an image-making ceremony; you will not merely be creating pictures and observing them, but becoming emotionally involved, getting excited, literally invoking the god of the seas himself. Particular images will not feel right, however, but you will know immediately when you have captured a suitable image as it will feel comfortable as you open up the appropriate response, though for some it may be necessary to perform a kind of mental dress rehearsal in order to discover exactly what does feel right. Our gut reaction to pieces of music, emotive song lyrics, visual forms of art, etc., signal to us whether or not we find them appealing and easy to admit into consciousness and it is this function upon which one calls during visualisation, the part of the psyche that says either 'I like', or 'I don't like', or what academic psychology blandly calls the right-brain function. Whatever you are visualising for, get emotional about it and feel the joy of having created something in your mind that may come to pass any day now. You do really want this thing you are visualising for, don't you?

The 'behave as if' technique permeates not only the unconscious mode of operation, working upon the individual, but reaches the universal level to bring changes in the environment, that is, apart from its immediate physical effect, transformations occur at an external level as a result of this process: the unseen hand of God? To quote Emerson again, 'Every act rewards itself . . . first in the thing, or in real nature; and secondly in the circumstance, or in apparent nature.' So it is as if during this operation the unconscious says, 'Oh well, this is what must be happening (at the sensation level), let's create more of the appropriate conditions,' for it tends to swallow whole whatever is suggested to it.

One particular story, concerning a client for whom I performed a birth chart reading, exemplifies the workings of this mind game. My client had read nothing concerning self-help psychology but stumbled on the principle 'by accident', for during a severe bout of depression he was suddenly struck by this crazy idea which, as he later sardonically remarked, was like 'sticking two fingers up at the devil'. In spite of his dark mood and pent-up frustration, the thought occurred that he should act the way he would normally act when he was happy as it had long since become obvious that the black dog, pernicious beast that it is, cannot simply be disgorged as one might remove a splinter from a finger. He would henceforth greet people with a smile, instead of barely acknowledging them, enquire after their well being and actively participate in the present conversation instead of remaining conspicuously silent. Slowly, almost imperceptibly, he began to experience the psychological effects of being happy just so long as he did not return to dwelling upon the depression. Indeed, the more he persisted with this 'cunning charade' (his words, not mine), the more did the unconscious execute the idea as a reality, not being able to tell the difference between truth and charade.

'Go, but tell no man' is a poignant admonition to bear in mind when using 'As If' for more distant objectives such as (and I think it would be safe to assume that these represent the general quota of individual wants) the new car, the better paid job, the VCR, the attractive wife or providing husband. Keep your desire a secret and guard it well, as strenuously as you would protect your daughter from the onslaught of some approaching madman; not only does a fool and his money soon go separate ways, but a fool and his dream, if he doesn't keep it to himself. Simply disregard the present reality and persist in creating an atmosphere of 'having already got', though this technique is not to be played out for the benefit of friends and associates, for in indiscriminately broadcasting one's goals, despite having good friends, one invariably attracts thoughts from others that are out of harmony with one's own mental field. This is not necessarily so much a matter of others envy, resentment or more likely incredulity, as it is a simple attraction of the opposites in nature, for whenever there is an expression of a particular nature, the world is compelled to set up a complementary reaction — complementary as far as the universe is concerned, at least.

Fundamentally, the idea with 'As If' is to make an impression upon and thus activate the unconscious forces; remember the advice oft quoted by many a rich, up and coming go-getter: 'You don't have to *have* a million dollars, just *look* like a million dollars,' for there are few sweeter feelings than having accomplished some long cherished dream, and verily I say unto thee, with the right actions these feelings can be experienced now, albeit synthetically. And I make no apologies for perhaps making these ideas sound a little insane for that reaction would be symptomatic of the way in which the lopsided conscious ego clings to only that which it can see. The unconscious sees things differently, however, and we shall continue this exploration of the psyche with the ramifications of the fifth and final commandment, 'Thou Shalt Have Faith . . .', in the part that follows.

APPROACHING THE MAGICIAN'S WAND

The impersonal source of creative unfoldment with which one enters into communion during visualisation holds one rule for all, which is why it is necessary to proceed in a particular way, taking certain steps so that the universe will respond to your petitions. The wand which you hold whilst imaging is only a part of the creative process of the mental universe, a principle that is intrinsically altogether unconcerned about your ungranted wishes, your emotional breakdowns, your anger hostility, depression and endless Faustian nightmares. Why should it be? Consider the time-honoured adage, 'laugh and the world laughs with you . . .' within the context of the workings of universal mind: the verb here, 'laugh', can be substituted by any other word that pertains to an opening up to the flow of inner energies, so that one becomes a medium for the expression of life. This kind of openness to life, therefore other people, is seen most often in those whom we like to call successful, those who appear to be managing the art of living rather well, often without being aware of the fact, yet they are participating most gracefully with the unconscious as they possess a forward-looking attitude that makes way for the emergence of new life. This lifeward tendency of the unconscious cannot be arrested without suffering the usual consequences: rail at the universe and you do it alone.

As I have already indicated, becoming angry at life is something that falls upon deaf ears as far as the universal mind is concerned and I realise all too well that it is only human to expect that your desires should be vindicated sooner or later: 'At least life could provide something that I want,' I hear you complain. Yet this is precisely the kind of attitude that acts as the stumbling block between visualiser and the rest of life, and must be dispensed with if one is to take part successfully as an effective cocreator in one's universe. I have met this many times in people who, having visualised in earnest, soon came to feel the eroding streams of discouragement because 'nothing had happened'. Do we really expect the ocean to part at the sight of our wonderful feet? One acts more as a vessel for creative life when the distinction between human nature and Mother Nature has been clearly seen, understood and made use of. Life goes on regardless of the little mortal, yet the human ego will insist on having power, moulding everything into a shape befitting its own particular viewpoint so that its view of the world represents the whole of reality as it is in itself. In order to prolong this game so that the individual be in the 'right', petty arguments, beligerent assertions, fighting and sometimes war must be engaged in.

The conflict between the personal, all too human view of life (such as typically parochial thinking, negative emotions, lack of vision) and the way in which life actually manifests needs to be resolved if we are to be successful in the long run with our visualisations, for the problem for many lies not in the imaging sessions themselves, but in our heads whilst our plan is percolating. For those who set a visualisation in motion and then go out into the world expecting it to suddenly and miraculously turn up in the flesh are still living with this conflict and must realise that on the inner level, things are not quite the same as the outer, and Mother Nature will transform those energies into the physical in her own good time. In *Studies in Alchemy*, Mark L. Prophet remarks on this dichotomy: 'It must be realised that the exercise of control over matter is no ordinary process. The methods of alchemy can be simply stated and easily absorbed, but its precepts require the practice of a master artist. Nevertheless, results can come forth in diverse ways if the student will at least begin to try.' And of course there is our concept of time to consider; perhaps you feel that three months is quite long enough for the materialisation of your goal, another 'all too human attitude', and you would expect some results when that time has passed, but that is like trying to trap the wind in a cage, since one cannot impose limits upon something that by its very nature refuses to be limited. Many visualisations manifest spontaneously, although with our prior cooperation, so how are we to tell precisely when the result will occur? How, indeed.

The overriding difference between the natural processes of unfoldment and the way in which the human being attempts to grow is the temptation of possessiveness, the desiring for something permanent and lasting, for we have a propensity to become attached to people, situations, our favourite jacket, our job in the factory, and a host of other examples we tend to get used to and are reluctant to give up. The unfortunate consequence, for us, is that fate, God, nature, Cosmic Intelligence, etc., brings changes that we find problematic, though this has never been a problem to nature as it is quite content to break down an existing structure, let it decay, sweep away the debris and reproduce new energies in order for life to take form. This is a fact no-one can escape, yet we continue to cling to the old form in spite of the self-damage we may be doing. In recognising this dichotomy, it will be seen that there are particular ingrained human attitudes that are unworkable as far as living is concerned because the universe does not operate in those ways. The creative principle of the universe works towards the unfoldment of new life, leaving the deadwood behind, thus thoughts that are not aligned to this movement (those which attempt to shut out the world, make no allowance for changes in one's life and are not imbued with the desire to move on) coalesce and become part of this deadwood, metamorphosing into the flesh of one's own experiences — those stagnant, dull, oppressive situations. The life contained within us wants to be lived, one way or another, and when we avoid using it, its more unattractive half uses us instead.

It is worth stressing to the visualiser that, even though the requisite techniques may have been followed faithfully, to expect dramatic results in which God turns up with the goodies on the doorstep all too readily, is courting trouble. Should temporary deprivation of the given goal provoke any form of discouragement, the visualiser ought to open up as many avenues that may lead to the end result as is possible, and not let a desirous heart sink if the first portent of good fortune turns out to be a cul-de-sac. Certainly the Universal Mind is responding in its own silent and unhurried way, and either it is allowed to work according to its own nature — in the same manner that one would not try to interfere with the body's internal digestive processes — or the visualiser becomes exasperated at each twist and turn when the goal is eluded. Actively seeking out one's goal is fine, only if one is prepared to accept that today's actions may not yield the actual fruit one is searching for; it could arise from so many different sources, not necessarily the ones you had conceived of. Not only does the cooperation of the individual's free will help to create a spirit of accomplishment, in that the visualiser feels some way has been gone towards realising a dream, but it encourages the unconscious to steer one in the appropriate direction in a way that thinking never could. For this reason, I am not over fond of the ramblings of certain writers who advocate little more than sitting back and waiting for the pot of gold to drop from the skies, especially since this rather ambivalent state of affairs, commonly referred to as being asleep at the wheel, is known to have produced some rather undesirable consequences.

Any magical work deals with the fundamental energies present in nature that tend to build up and find their way into the environment of the individual as an event. Thus when no channels are created for the emergence of these forces, the energy (because it must manifest) will break out through the least line of resistance. But because it has not been allowed to flow, this is usually a dissatisfying result, at worst a painful one. Unconscious attractions of the unsavoury variety are thus the work of inner forces transforming into an event via the nearest available route, and in many cases this has occurred simply because the visualiser was unwilling to act. For instance, I have listened to stories from people who had visualised a relationship whilst at the same time leaving all the gates that would normally permit its impending arrival, indefinitely shut. Many of them, after having employed the general techniques, were not prepared to take any action, either direct or indirect, in pursuit of the largely unknowable results, and when they came they did so abruptly and with a disappointing end. What they met with was not the makings of their ideal relationship with a suitor of the opposite sex, but a rather less attractive encounter with someone who had proferred themselves all too readily, offering nothing like the dream of their envisioned star-crossed romance. It was only then that they realised their visualisations had come true, but in circumstances which they felt necessary to resist because the other person was not 'right', or certain elements from the original imagings were missing. Nevertheless, the Universal Mind had delivered what had been asked for. Perhaps more action on the part of these disillusioned mortals would have brought them into contact with a situation that made the object of their desire more accessible. However, the saving grace for these examples is that they eventually found what they were looking for, as the unconscious remains committed to seeking out the goal. This is in the nature of the beast; unconscious energy is driven irresistibly under its own steam to attract its own likeness and, as we have seen, cannot be eclipsed by inactivity as sooner or later fate catches up with us — the reply of the Universal Mind. This reply comes through circumstances we have usually unconsciously attracted (as exemplified in the account at the end of Chapter Three), that is, with the thoughts we allow to roam through our mind, and it is these thoughts we must guard and attend to during the period between imaging ritual and the longed for result, for as we should not engage in poor visualisations, to the same extent we should not indulge in poor thinking.

The reactions to watch out for, born of negative emotional patterning, are: 'Nothing's happened after two months', 'Maybe visualising is just a fool's paradise', or 'I can't see how it might ever happen'. In the light of archetypal human affairs, the latter reaction is understandable when one considers the ego's propensity for demanding facts or details in order to be reassured of a safe future, a fact which is highlighted in the visits to the clairvoyant or medium, by countless people wondering just what the great spirit has in store for them. This desire to know precisely what is around the next corner or in the case of the visualiser to be comforted with the knowledge that it *will* happen can never be fulfilled because of the nature of the ego itself, because it cannot be in two places at once. How can a single focal point of consciousness possibly be aware of the whole panoramic view of reality? To draw an analogy, the attempt to know all of one's future is akin to viewing a very confined area of space through a telescope: you can only be aware of one piece of visual information at any one time and as soon as you move the telescope to another area, the previous one has disappeared, or at least that's what our eyes tell us. Likewise, the ego can never 'see how it might happen', but our heart may tell us otherwise.

But the issue might well be raised of how long one ought to continue with visualisations and this proves to be a rather ambiguous area, since it cannot be likened to that of the general practitioner's prescribed treatment of a certain number of days or weeks after which one's maladies will be cured. However, a period of approximately two months is a reliable average in order to infuse the unconscious with sufficient weight, though it goes without saying that the longer one continues, the more powerful will it affect the inner mind. Sometimes, the individual is not required to use visualisation in order to attract from the outside, as in the case of intense desire where the results appear as a kind of chain reaction where one will acquire a vital piece of information related to one's goal, perhaps through a friend who can link you with someone else who just happens to know the person you need to see. Such is the nature of attraction, as it can be seen in retrospect that one's coincidental meeting seems too perfect a fit in the larger scheme of things, though to the person whose eyes are closed it is lucky. However, the majority of us mortals will fail to encourage nature to yield a little to our plans through simple desire, for the accompanying attitudes (for example, discouragement, doubt, incredulity) are the very things cutting away at the roots of the original desire, so that the plan never has time to germinate. Hence there exists the requirement for a structured technique that with a few exceptions can be applied by anyone from the proverbial person-off-the-street to the adept occultist, for even in the case of the latter, as far as Mother Nature is concerned, he or she is simply another mortal. Despite familiarity with her laws, she holds no favourites.

In utilising this enigmatic, unseen force, no different in kind from Merlin's wand (except that the human model is unable to produce such instant results), I urge you to take note of the commandments laid out in this chapter and strenuously apply them. The secrets of nature are bound up in the relationship between mind and matter and our time-honoured, antiquated methods of unlocking the answers are effective only with those who are capable of receiving them and are aware that the life flowing invisibly through them calls forth its correspondent wherever they may go. This is why visualisation is such a potent oracle, as it determines much of what will be, not because of divine plan or design (although it could be asked whether we are fated to visualise!), but because the individual has deemed it to be so. In fact one is better off for using visualisation; with its efficacy we can become successful cocreators in our universe since we are thus geared more effectively to the universe's laws of attraction.

CHAPTER 6
RITUAL INTENTIONS — HEALTH, LOVE AND WEALTH

Pictures speak truths to the heart that said another way, would fall upon deaf ears.

Before proceeding to the following guided journeys through inner space, I would like to discuss the imagined forms themselves and the role they play in activating the mostly unknowable unconscious forces. Undoubtedly, the images which animatedly sprang to life under the will of consciousness bear a strong relationship to the visualiser's realised goal, yet they rarely tend to be an identical replica, in spite of the painstaking details that the neophyte has etched into the rituals. In certain occult quarters we are led to believe that once an image is formed in the mind, an exact reprint appears on the astral plane which then begins to clothe itself with thought energy (the 'descension of the planes' theory) until the astral form becomes denser and denser, and lo and behold does it appear on the material plane. Yet despite whatever truths may be lurking in this theory, I am unable to hold with the idea that an astral double is responsible for the materialisation of envisioned goals, for as is so often the case, the actual events that transpire do not correlate exactly with the images in ritual, although it is nonetheless the preceding images that have influenced the actual physical manifestations. Thus, if the actual mental pictures themselves are not replicated in physical life, they can at least be said to possess sufficient force as a symbolic representation of the objects to which they are directed.

This idea, then, simplifies matters as far as the images themselves are concerned, for it is the vessel into which they fall, that is the unconscious, that holds the intelligence to bring about a situation in which the inner imagined scenes can be replayed. However, some writers have referred to the imagined forms as a matrix into which thought energy is poured, yet I am inclined to opt for a rather different analogy if one considers a mental image as nothing other than simply that. If it is fundamentally a thought creation that gathers an energy force around it, by virtue of a feeling association, and then begins to assume form within the inner mind, setting up a kind of psychic magnet, then I feel one might come fairly close to the truth of what really happens in the interplay between thought and event. Yet the power of inner images is nonetheless for being just that at the onset of visualisation, for they are the first stage in a sequence of inner events.

In order to delve further into this little matter, I would like to take the opportunity to dislodge the safe preconceptions of those who take the material world as the final word. The solid objects surrounding you and I, are not solid after all: their most fundamental, essential make-up is composed of a force, or energy or rather the composition *is* energy *per se*. The quantum factor of the new physics will startle the hard-nosed materialist who insists that their Chesterfield settee is really an inanimate object. The physicist may describe such an article as a mass concentrated energy; focus enough energy into one particular space and matter appears — does this not sound like the process of manifestation in visualisation? Perhaps unwittingly, Messrs Bohm, Einstein, Bohr and company have provided a badge of acceptability for occult matters, for their *scientific* findings point towards the realities of the inner worlds and the ephemerality of nature. They are also in keeping with the nature of a manifested visualisation, whereby the actual object that at last appears on the material plane does not necessarily correspond identically to the original image, for the essence of the quantum factor is one of chance and unpredictability whereby atoms refuse to hold to a specified path. Thus, while I hold that mind is the ultimate cause of such a manifestation, there exists an X factor that leaves an element of chance as to the exact nature of the finished replica as it enters one's life. (Student visualisers please do not despair, visualisation always works, but don't assume that you've gone wrong when your manifestation on this plane is not an exact copy of your scenarios on the inner one.)

This revelation from our relations in the world of quantum physics is what makes my 'essence' theory more digestible. It works like this: If I visualise for a car, projecting its image on my inner screen, the 'essence' of that car (imagined form) is directly related to the 'essence' of the actual, objective car. If the physical universe is nothing other than energy, with its multitude of different forms vibrating at different rates from the subtle (thought, emotions, electricity) to the dense (physical body) to the extremely dense (minerals, metals), then the 'essence' of the object which we seek to attract is directly related to the energies we have set into motion whilst visualising for it. Expressed the other way around, some of the subtle forces engineered during ritual (astral forces, psychological energies or vibrations) are eventually caught up in the forces, or energies which form the nucleus of the physical object to which the ritual is aimed, and in this I include what we have termed inanimate objects. One could almost say that in visualising for a car, one *becomes* that car, for the energies one brings about within the psyche in that particular ritual, are the same in kind as the essence of the solid, objective car. This is the force which lies behind the technique of creating a living reality from one's desired goal, the attempt to become one with it, for one only attracts what is already a part of that self.

HEALTH

This heading is simply an umbrella which covers anything related to self-development, inner emotional healing, self-confidence, contentment with one's lot in life, in fact anything that promotes a feeling of well being. It may be that the reader would be more attracted to the following two sections, as it is typical of modern people to want to attract 'stuff' from the outside. There is always the desire to have rather than to be, and that desire signifies a common lack of knowledge of the mind. Yet the work must first be performed on the inner self, for one cannot attract and continue to make 'work' creatively (i.e. handle successfully) something that is not already a part of one's own psyche already. Can the obnoxious and cynical person ever handle a loving relationship successfully if they use the requisite techniques in order to attract a partner, as laid out in the subsequent part?

It is for this reason that Health, Love, Wealth are placed in this order, and for a significant psychological reason: the sequence of these three motivations begins within the subject and moves towards the object. One's psychological health is the prime matter, and the support system is not to be found in outer objects, for they can never, ultimately, bring lasting inner peace and security. Creative imagination is a powerful healing tool for even the most depressed person, though inner peace must be worked at (and perhaps never absolutely 'achieved', for achievement suggests finality, an end) by examining hidden fears and those inner motivations which would deny action. Thus the first exercise is to promote faith in the inner worlds, confidence in one's self-expression and conviction within one's words. We must possess faith in our views and decisions, faith in our ability to act and forge ahead, but, at a more sublime level, faith in ourselves as human beings.

What follows is a series of guided imageries devoted to the psychological health of the individual, though as with the psychiatrist's counselling session, their effectiveness is entirely dependent on the individual who attempts to make use of them. The essays are intended as a broad outline to enclose what may commonly be used in visualisation, and of course may be altered considerably by the visualiser to suit his or her particular situation in life. It will be useful to record the text of the following visualisations on tape, reading them at an appropriately slow pace, so that when they are played back, and you practise forming the images, there is time for them to form and develop. Let us commence.

You are lying in a deserted field on a warm, sunny day where not a sound can be heard except perhaps for the occasional birdsong. You are looking up into the sun; observe its shape, its golden colour, sense its powerful and penetrative rays being absorbed as you draw its essence into you. Now that life-giving golden orb is above your chest; acknowledge its power to animate your being as it sinks inside you, filling your body with a rich, warming and purifying light — and at that moment you *are* that sun. That same creative power you feel possessed of in your heart, its dynamic heat beginning to enliven and invigorate as its rays stretch toward every part of your body. Your eyes are opened to the light emanating from your heart centre, pulsating across your chest, down your arms, down towards your abdomen and finally travelling down both legs until it reaches your feet. As you remain in this state with your own personal sun projecting a beautiful golden aura through your body, you begin to feel a tingling sensation; a subtle energising force is beginning to create rhythms through the whole of your bodily network and you slowly begin to feel more energetic, vigorous, powerful, magnetic. You realise that you have within you, part of the universe, a creative force empowered to attract joyous living.

You have just awoken from a pleasant night's sleep. With your alarm clock showing 7:30 a.m., a shaft of sunlight creeps across the bedroom wall through the orange curtains. After the initial bleary-eyed yawn, you throw back the bedclothes and rush to open the curtains; you have never felt more alive than at this point for you have so many things to feel glad about, so many tasks to accomplish, friends to meet, places to visit. You feel a warm, healthy glow as the smile appears on your face yet again, encouraged by the view from your bedroom window. The rising sun spreads a beautiful light over the fields stretching into the distance and you recall that sun once again as a magnificent symbol of what is found inside of you — when you care enough to look for it.

You are observing your reflection in the bathroom mirror. Notice the colour and shape of your eyes, your features, the shape of your nose and lips, the way your hair is arranged. Continuing with this observation, you break out in a big, genuine smile that instantly transforms your whole aura and now you are radiating good health, vitality, strength, courage and willpower. You feel as if your confidence has increased tenfold, simply because of that one smile; it's a strange feeling, a sense of magnanimous power that could draw towards you anything that you so desired. That feeling has been aroused without any thinking on your part, it simply came into existence, born from that inner centre which is your heart, the sun. As you continue to study that splendid image before you, the faith in your heart for today seems to grow still stronger, accelerating and rapidly moving you to such a wonderful feeling that it belies the words to describe it. You watch your lips move as you say these words, 'Today is my very best day, thank God I'm alive.'

LOVE

Love is as subjective as the ground we stand upon whilst observing the world, but love in itself, I believe, is open to an objective definition. If, as the Polish proverb says, 'The greatest love is a mother's . . .', then it comes pretty close to a universal definition on the nature of loving, for the true mother love is that which asks for nothing in return. In real love, I do not love someone because of the way they look, how much money they spend on me or the affection that is reciprocated, I love them simply because they are there, because it's part of my nature to love the essence of that person, what emanates from them. Herein lies the enigma of attraction, and this is possibly the closest approximation one will ever arrive at for an objective description of love.

The heading of 'Love' for this ritual covers all manner of human relating and this is the second phase in our self-development scheme. In the first, we paid necessary attention to the inner core of psychological security upon which the ego must rest, however precariously. Now we find the human need to relate, to seek life in others outside of the self, which brings me to the reason as to *why* one seeks to bring the object of one's dreams into one's life. We are accustomed to hearing colloquial expressions about someone special, 'Mr Right', that certain someone, as if there was a perfect person that existed specially for us. These ideals are born out of the deeply felt hope that such a person is out there, and when we actually meet him, or her, all of our troubles will magically disappear as we sail off hand in hand into the dusky scarlet sunset. In short we believe wholly that such a relationship will make us happy, which is fine insofar as some individual responsibility is assumed, for relationships require effort, if only the effort at understanding. Using visualisation to attract a partner certainly works, though (like certain literature I have seen with directives for bringing back a strayed husband), I would advise against using this particular ritual to draw some actual known person towards you.

And then of course there are so many different types of love: there is sexual love, where the passions are aroused through a mutual enjoyment of each other's bodies; romantic love, when we feel ourselves to be under the spell of a heavenly Eros (whilst in fact, a part of ourselves has been activated and caught up in the love object); the caring and sharing kind of love where the partners meet each other on a one-to-one basis; maternal/paternal love; love of another's talents and gifts; love of another's money, and so on. For the following guided scenarios, and I stress that they represent only a blueprint for your own visualisations, prepare by creating a mind's eye of the picture of the ideal partner, lover, boyfriend, girlfriend or whatever. You will have no need to labour strenuously in deciding what kind of relationship you feel suited to, if you *need* a partner badly enough, you will know already. If you have to sit around thinking about the type of partner you require, then you are most likely not ready for a long-term partnership with a member of the opposite (or same) sex.

(N.B. The rituals for this section are presented with the feminine gender, i.e. they are directed towards a male reader using visualisation to attract a female. It goes without saying that the female reader would simply reverse the genders.)

You see before you closely a face, and only that face, nothing else appears in the background, and even if it does, it fades into insignificance next to the image that is now looking back at you. Observe closely the shape, the colour of the eyes and hair, the length of hair, the shape of the lips and nose. This female (male) face is a symbolic picture of the feminine (masculine) archetype present within you, that is, an image of all that is appealing in a woman, qualities in the object which stir and enchant because some of those traits exist within. [To elucidate further, I would recall Christian Nestell's illuminating quote on the enigma of attraction, 'The beauty seen is partly in him who sees it', in other words, whatever is not inherently a part of us, cannot attract us to that quality in someone else.]

As the image forms before you, it slowly begins to animate, to come alive and you begin to realise that she is a living being, and you can hear the unspoken words of love coming directly from her, a strange feeling that lets you know she is more than a mere picture. She smiles a radiant, endearing smile as you reach out to touch her face; you touch her cheeks, feel the softness of her hair, her lips, and sense the reality of her existence. You know that she exists for you and it feels wonderful. The longer you continue to be with her, the stronger does the feeling become and the sensation is truly marvellous. Here you are with your ideal, cherished love object.

You and your lover are on holiday, walking hand in hand along the beach as the sun begins its slow descent over the horizon. Both of you pause to observe the magnificent sight of this great scarlet orb sinking, as if into the sea, as the evening sky with its tapestry of clouds becomes a shade more dark. You turn to look at her and she smiles lovingly at you, you know in your heart that her eyes are saying, 'I love you', and you feel only love, a deeply-felt inexplicable bliss, when you are by her side. You continue to walk along the sands, just the two of you, then you stop to observe your reflections in a nearby pool. You become transfixed at the images looking back at you. Here you are with your lover on this warm and dusky summer evening sharing each other's presence, feeling her close to you. It could almost be a mirage but there is the evidence in that pool of water.

It is morning and you awaken in your hotel bedroom and you open your eyes to the sight of your lover, still sleeping. Somehow she seems even more beautiful like this: peaceful, angelic, untouched by the spoils of daily living, almost vulnerable, in fact. You simply want to look at her right now, the way her long hair falls carelessly about the pillow, how she seems almost childlike and kittenish with her eyes closed. You stroke her shoulder and run your finger along her soft skin as you watch her still sleeping, then, as she opens her eyes and looks up at you, her face is transformed with the most tender, loving smile you could ever wish to receive. As she beckons with open arms, you embrace and feel her warmth around you, enclosed as in a gentle river on a summer's day, experiencing a feeling of love and warmth like you've never felt before. As you hold this embrace a little longer, the emotions stirring in you generate a feeling of tranquility, contentment, fullness and joy as you perceive a pure harmony, the effect of being at one with yourself, with your loved one, and with the universe.

WEALTH

Ah, who wouldn't visualise for more money in this present age of economic instability, and the spectre of unemployment creeping up on too high a percentage of the general population? Who wouldn't visualise themselves with a six-figure bank balance, a house in the country, a car that always starts first time and dispenses tequila Sunrises, and a career so well paid that the Inland Revenue has a field day with your gross earnings? In spite of this suggested promise of opulence as a result of visualisation, it pays to bear in mind the advice of Ophiel and begin humbly, especially those who are the so-called students of visualisation. If you are going to make the acquisition of material possessions your thing, then I suggest that you begin with objects that require little handling, that is, items which do not entail large responsibilities. So much depends upon the individual, and how well versed he or she is in the art of visualisation. A well-practised visualiser may be so in tune with the universe that a bid for material things of a high value can be made and the individual be able to receive them quite well indeed. I would imagine that anyone new to the subject of mind power may simply have one specific material item in mind, say, a video-cassette recorder, or a car, or simply a well-paid job and with enough energy focused upon that one particular object, the goal ought to be realised fairly easily.

As students of the occult progress and their understanding of the inner worlds increases, the accent on possessions diminishes and acquisitiveness takes a back seat. This does not mean, however, that they become totally unconcerned with the material world, in fact their general standard of living probably improves as their knowledge of the universe is expanded and the underlying realities concerning matter made clearer. Quite simply, money and its acquisition becomes less of a problem since they are able to attract it easier. How might this come about? If the outer environment, which naturally includes possessions, is a symbol of one's inner world in that it mirrors the state of one's psyche, and one finds the happily married man surrounded by the comforts of material wealth, then one may reasonably assume a relative proportion of 'wealth' to exist on the inner plane. Those symbols of material prosperity — the grand rambling mansion, the most expensive furniture one can buy, the platinum jewellery, the Diners Club card — are the outgrowth of wealth accumulating on the inner level; the inner sense of grandeur, a positive sense of self-worth that has made a person of great value in monetary terms because they value themselves on the interior, soul level. It is the theme of intangible object transforming itself into actual physical object.

The phenomenon is perhaps made clearer when one considers the astrological birth chart; the 'second house' of a natal chart is connected with those material possessions with which we surround ourselves for the purpose of security, but as the horoscope is fundamentally a network of psychological energies it cannot refer to any specific object on the outer plane. Furthermore, the essence of the second house is concerned with intangibles such as a sense of self-worth, values and the general desire nature of the human being — the attitudes towards possessing something, not the possessed object. Here is where the link between one's self-esteem and the inner attributes one values, and the type of possessions (and amount of money) one acquires shows up, for what one values consciously in the objects before the eyes is a symbolic act of unconsciously appreciating 'something' about one's inner self or soul, and indeed, life in general. Thus, the person who values themselves as a human being, who is prosperous in heart and soul, shall have little need to strain against the environment to make a dollar, for they shall attract wealth by virtue of 'being'. Or by visualisation. The following guided tours of the inner landscapes serve as a suggested plan as to what one might hope to achieve in visualisations for material objects.

As you are shown into the manager's office you are greeted with a sincere smile and warm handshake and immediately you warm to the manager's open, cordial manner. You have prepared little for this interview for your improved self-image and positive, direct assertiveness will impress your future boss as to the kind of person you are; the only preparations you have performed are specific details relating to the nature of the work itself. You know that this is a job you can easily handle, even if you haven't done exactly the same kind of work before. As you discuss the requirements related to this position, you find yourself speaking with complete confidence and a relaxed easy-going manner, though knowledgeable and authoritative. The manager listens approvingly, following your every word with an occasional nod of the head and, as you continue your discourse, the manager's gestures indicate pleasure at what you say.

At the midpoint of the interview the manager begins to give out signals which suggest to you that you are the person required for the job, a sign compounded by the manager asking as to whether or not the present salary is acceptable and looking almost relieved as you reply, 'Yes, it seems quite fair.' After relaying more details connected with the position, the manager pauses and sits back, studiously looking over your application form on the desk. During this interim period you watch the manager's face and can see the plain satisfaction expressed there. Then the manager rises, offers an outstretched hand again, and as you both shake on it, you hear those magic words, 'I'm pleased to welcome you to the organisation; you've got the job.'

You are on your way home from your new job. This has been your first week and you are looking forward to the extra money being deposited into the bank, although the real feeling of contentment comes from knowing that you will now have much more *freedom*. The freedom to be able to say, 'I don't *have* to put up with second best anymore; if I want to take the train first class, I can, I deserve it.' You pull your first wage slip out of your pocket and look at the net amount, and you think to yourself: *'I did it, I passed the interview with flying colours and I got the job!* Now I can spend money on those expensive items I've wanted for so long, buy generous birthday presents and have ample left to put away for saving.' The feeling within tells you that you know how to live prosperously, that you deserve to live life first class and exude wealth, after all, here is the evidence of your own senses, the fulfilment of your material world. What a prosperous soul you are!

AN AFTERWORD

A friend once suggested the words, 'Making Your Dreams Come True' for the title of this book, as in its embryonic form it was to be a kind of potpourri of mind-power techniques designed to set the reader on the magical road to success. But I resisted. Principally, because of the simplicity it evoked, but mainly because (bearing in mind what the notion of success-with-mental-images may suggest to the unaware individual with its connotations of something-for-nothing) it had long ago occured to me that the richer, more profound aspects of visualisation ought to be brought to the reader's attention. Needless to say, only a fool would entertain the idea of getting something for nothing.

After having used visualisation techniques to attract specific 'objects' a curious thing happened to me, in the style of a Zen paradox: I discovered that those cherished items I visualised for were, in the end, valueless when compared with the inner wisdom I uncovered about the workings of the psyche. That is, the attraction of material pleasures (via this little technique called visualisation) served as the process by which I discovered that such external charms are transitory. But I *had* to pursue them in order to discover that I did not in fact, deep down, want to pursue them. Hence, a shift in values came about.

Thus, the more sublime intention of the book is to inspire self-awareness in the reader, however, visualisation merely happens to be a technique, a catalyst that may set the process in motion. In this way, visualisation may be seen as an indirect, accidental method of coming to an awareness of Self, for when one has seen beyond its more superficial uses, the dawn of self-realisation begins to emerge and something more meaningful happens. But you may well ask, 'Precisely what do you mean by "self-awareness", "the dawn of self-realisation"?' Well, let us suppose that you proceed with a visualisation for nothing more profound than a compact-disc player and lo and behold, through the laws of attraction, you find yourself availed of such a marvellous piece of technology as this. In your great satisfaction that visualisation actually works, you desire more of the same kind of results with your clever efforts of the imagination. So far, so good.

However, somewhere along this line of pursuit you would be asking yourself the question oft repeated by many occultists: how does it work? Yet it is the question that is important, regardless of whether one is able to provide an answer, or whether one looks for it in the world outside or the world within. For it is the commencement of this self-analysis, such as wondering just how it comes about, that imagining something intensely can make it happen, that yields more and more questions, each one becoming successively more profound and subtle. Eventually, it is hoped that an individual will have come to an appreciation of their place in the universe, i.e. their relationship to the rest of life.

As I pointed out in the introduction, visualisation still sometimes seems (to me) like a minor miracle, but in time the miraculousness becomes less and less pronounced, to be replaced by the sobering knowledge that one has witnessed a perfectly ordinary process that belongs to Nature herself. Experience of successful materialisations opens the portals to the creative potential of the unconscious mind, and when one has ceased to be so amazed at its power (a typical reaction of the rational mind) one acquires the wisdom to see that mind is everywhere and one's rituals have been the transformation of one kind of energy into another. Nothing too miraculous about that.

One particular, simple aim of the book is to encourage people to live more successful lives — nothing more — and visualisation serves as a practical method by which one may experience the powers of mind first hand, in addition to being a relatively easy thing to do. Perhaps, sentimentally speaking, the book is my sincere effort to share something wonderful with the reader. It strikes me that too few of us are aware of the capacity for creative power invested within, and I hope that by now you have been sufficiently encouraged to introduce mind-power techniques into your daily living.

I expect, though, that much resistance to the magical world within will persist due to insistence that ultimate reality must lie in the object, in the world directly perceived with the senses. This view of reality works only in areas where an objective, reliable conclusion can be made, for attempting a logical appraisal of a part of reality that, by its very nature, does not lend itself to logic (dreams, emotions, the unconscious) is to fall short of truly representing it. For example, many offerings from writers of occult material must speak in terms of *causing* something to happen (with the mind) whereby one agency affects another by its acting

114

upon it, and indeed, this is the type of language I have used myself throughout the book. This principle is more readily entertained by the Western mind than that of 'affecting by non-action'. But, and perhaps it serves as an irony, one can hardly speak of non-action if the mind is supposed to be a creative, active force, for I do not believe that visualisation actually causes anything to happen, as Newtonian physics would have it, but awakens that part of the mind that somehow knows where our goal is to be found and directs us accordingly. And who is to say that that knowledge must necessarily be logical? Relative to this theme I quote Rainer Maria Rilke: 'The future enters into us; in order to transform itself in us, long before it happens.'

That there is a magical world within is inconceivable to those with no direct access to it, but that is only because their egos refuse to look there, so I dedicate *Applied Visualisation* to those earnest students of life who would attempt to improve their lot out of an inner thirst to live a meaningful, prosperous life, and especially to those who have been forced to look inward by the (some say necessary) cold hand of despair and discouragement. An acknowledgement of failure is painful indeed, yet to come to terms with oneself and realise that, despite past frustrations, one's inner fire and passion for living has not diminished is to encounter that 'something' within, crying out for its unlived life. To these individuals in particular are the successful living exhortations dedicated — perhaps because some of my own past can be gleaned in them.

Lastly, I remember reading an advertisement spread somewhere for the (then) current catalogue of David Bowie albums, bearing the slogan (in several other languages): 'Tomorrow belongs to those who can hear it coming,' which, if one substitutes 'see' for 'hear', forms what I believe to be a rather fitting aphorism for those to whom this book is dedicated. As I indicated at the beginning, the practice of visualisation and ritual magic requires a somewhat special attitude, or more appositely, for it to work

effectively, the attitude of a particular or special consciousness. And the 'tomorrow' referred to above is that bright
day where one may arrive at a deeper understanding of Self.
Instead of needing to attract more fortunate circumstances
one will bring them about quite unintentionally, for one will
have changed inwardly too. So if tomorrow belongs to those
who can see it coming, it is because they have dared to
believe in a richer, more satisfying way of life, to have held
on to their dream in order that it should come true. Perhaps
I should have stuck with the original title. The last words on
the subject for this chapter I leave to Daniel H. Burnham:
'Make no little plans; they have no magic to stir men's
blood . . . make big plans, aim high in hope and work.'

CHAPTER 7
TEN-WEEK 'WORK OUT'

As a further incentive towards making one's dreams come true, what follows is a detailed, step-by-step visualisation programme, taking you from the basics of relaxation up to the special kinds of attitude necessary to a successful imaging ritual. The early parts may seem a little tedious, yet I advise that you carry them out and persevere, for the experience thus gained is going to prove invaluable. Weeks three to five are the beginnings of imaging proper, commencing with basic exercises and rounding off with a more animated and lifelike kind of visualisation.

So as not to bore the novice visualiser into abandoning the 'course' and taking up piano lessons or karate instead, week six sees the inception of one's very own Goal Setting Programme, no less than a visualise-your-way-to-success plan. The techniques I have laid out throughout the book are standard to any occultist/magician/'positive thinker' (or whatever), but whether or not one successfully *applies* these techniques is left up to individual effort. However, if manna does not shower upon one from heaven after the first two months, this does not necessarily mean that the visualisation has 'failed'. If one wants to view the non-appearance (so far) of the envisaged object as a failure then go ahead, but the mistake here would be in imposing a time limit on such an undertaking, and the only words of advice I could impart in this situation would be, 'continue to believe in your desired dream, for if you are visualising strongly enough for it you shall have it sooner or later — this is in the nature of the beast.'

The exercises here are to be performed no less than five days per week (seven, preferably), initially perhaps for a period of fifteen minutes, though it is to be hoped that as week six arrives, the sessions will have lengthened out to at least half an hour. If you will persist with the relaxation exercises then it follows that your visualisation will prove more effective but if you must skip the relaxation section then move directly on to the exercises for basic imagery. If this still proves tedious to you, then you could always take up karate.

WEEK ONE: RELAXATION

The basis of this two-week exercise is to get the mind into a relatively relaxed state, a task which, as you may have experienced, cannot always be accomplished by simply 'sitting back and taking it easy'. This is because if the body is subject to typical everyday tensions — the kind invoked by rush hour traffic, unexpected downpours of rain when it is highly inconvenient, or one of 'those days' — the mind cannot be expected to follow suit and acquiesce. Indeed, it is in this instance that we have a 'matter over mind' situation. Thus initially, it is the 'matter' which requires attention, and even if you consider yourself a 'laid back' kind of person, I recommend that you participate in these preparatory exercises.

The first and most fundamental requirement is to find a place where you can have total silence, and in this day and age, finding one is probably no mean feat in itself. It is for this reason that I suggest (as I have done so myself on numerous occasions) that you visualise late at night when there is at least a greater chance of having quietude from your environment. If you live alone then you have more freedom to set up imaging sessions; if you share a household, then you *must* arrange a time when you can either be alone completely, or at least be 'off by yourself', but whatever your situation, the two prerequisites to bear in mind are a) solitude, and b) quietude. Such is the stage-setting for visualisation.

In either a comfortable armchair or lying on your back (with arms loose), curl your toes as tightly as possible and hold this position for about ten seconds. During this time, become aware of the sensation of tension, of what it feels like — let go and relax, and then tense once more. On relaxing the second time you are to visualise 'streams' of tension leaving your feet and toes as you sense them becoming more and more relaxed. Simply let go and allow your feet to relax. The same technique may now be applied

119

to the muscles in your thighs — tense your thighs and visualise the release of energy as you relax — the muscles in your stomach, arms, shoulders and face. Simply tighten the muscles in these parts of your body for a duration of ten seconds, let go, and imagine a flow of tension/energy being 'spent' from that area of your body as you let go. Perform this exercise for not less than five days, say, for a duration of fifteen minutes.

Self-Analysis

Were you able to feel acutely, the transition from tensed to relaxed? Were you able to relax mentally more easily after having performed the exercise?

NB. If you are able to answer 'yes' to the questions in the Self-Analysis section, then consider yourself to be making suitable progress.

Points To Remember

Perform the exercises no less than five days per week.

WEEK TWO: RELAXATION

These exercises with various additions, are a continuation of the programme laid out in the previous week. It goes without saying that, provided that you have performed the exercise regularly, you will find it easier to relax by the beginning of the second week. Perhaps, also, you have felt encouraged enough to increase the frequency of the exercise, and indeed, the length?

In the position you have chosen to adopt, take in a good, long deep breath, filling your lungs as much as possible, and then slowly exhale. When you repeat this (now with your eyes closed), visualise those streams of energy/tension emanating from your whole body. (As this 'energy' is without physical form, though nonetheless real you could imagine it as either droplets, vibrations, a vapoury substance, or even coloured smoke.) Take in your deep breath *slowly* and exhale at the same rate whilst you 'see' the tension slowly easing away from your head, arms, chest, legs, and so forth. Continue for about five minutes in this manner, and your body will start to feel loose and relaxed. Next, return to the tension/relaxation sequence as outlined in week one, commencing with your toes and working eventually up to your face.

At this point in the exercise you ought to be feeling relatively loosened up, and the next stage in this three-part exercise is simply to heighten the experience, and to make a little more progress with your visualising. Beginning at your feet, imagine a small bright light shining upon your toes. It is not merely enough to 'see' this light; you must 'feel' it too — feel its warmth, its soothing effect as both feet begin to loosen up and relax. Persist with this part of the exercise until you can actually 'feel' the warmth from this glowing light upon your feet, a feat (no pun intended) made possible since, believe it or not, our so-called physical sensations are actually mental in origin.

Next, mentally direct this light so that it shines along the

121

length of your legs and repeat the process; feel how wonderfully relaxing it is to be bathed in this white light as your tension gradually eases away. As usual, this method can now be applied to the upper parts of the body: your arms, shoulders, hands, and face. Admittedly, these three exercises are going to last for longer than fifteen minutes, and if you prefer not to spend a great deal of time on relaxation techniques, then select just one exercise and carry that out for the standard quarter hour. (Preferably, the breathing exercise.)

Self-Analysis

Do you have a clear, strong image of the 'energy streams' leaving your body?
Have you begun to sense a kind of harmony between mind and body?
Do you feel more energetic after having completed the exercises?

Points To Remember

Exhale and inhale at the same rate during the breathing exercises in order to establish a positive rhythm.

A successful visualisation is contingent upon a harmonious mind–body relationship.

WEEK THREE: BASIC IMAGERY

We now enter into the realm of image making proper, but — and this applies as a standard rule for all of the exercises — one will not perform effectively if one is not at first relaxed, hence, Golden Rule Number One: make sure you are as relaxed as possible at the time. Perhaps ten minutes or so will be required prior to each exercise, during which you will utilise any of the three relaxation techniques given in week two, for I cannot stress enough that calmness of both mind and body are necessary preparations for so called mind-power rituals.

Our first real encounter with directed imagination will be that of simple, recognisable shapes, which you will create, with eyes closed, as an image in your consciousness. For example, form the image of a white circle upon a dark background (or vice versa, if you prefer) and see for how long you can hold it there, clearly and strongly. Whether or not you are gifted with a vivid imagination, retaining this one image for more than a few seconds may be more difficult than it first sounds hence, this week, the emphasis is upon *retaining* certain images within the mind's eye. This discipline you will find necessary when week six arrives, and you will be visualising for your own goal.

Practise with other two-dimensional images such as the square, triangle, and rectangle, making a conscious effort to see them clearly and well defined (perhaps against a contrasting background) but above all, attempt to retain them in that clear and well defined form. Resist the temptation to move on haphazardly from one image to the next without having firmly impressed the previous image upon your memory. Following on from this exercise, we may now move on to everyday three-dimensional objects in order to create a firm impression of them within the mind's eye. Look around your room and 'take in' any selected object (an armchair, television, reading lamp, telephone, coffee table, etc.) and make a mental photograph, transferring it to your

123

memory and seeing it only in your imagination. In your mind's eye, take note of every little detail — its shape, size, dimensions, colour, etc. — and, again, practise holding on to the image for as long as is possible, repeating the exercise until you manage a fair measure of success. Again, the duration of the exercises ought to run to at least fifteen minutes.

Self-Analysis

Do you find that you are able to create those shape images much easier — that is, with much less effort — at the end of this week's exercise?

Points To Remember

The images you impress upon your mind's eye must possess detail, clarity, and to all intents and purposes appear as 'real' as the object they represent.

With sufficient repetition of this process, the exercise will become much easier as your memory will simply 'replay' to you, what has hitherto been impressed upon it.

WEEK FOUR:
ACTIVE IMAGINATION

Hopefully, by this stage, you will have become not just a little skilled in controlling at will, elements of your imagination necessary to a complete visualisation ritual. Also, it is to be hoped that you will have extended your exercise period as you become more proficient, and consequently, a little more encouraged. However, owing to the nature of last week's exercises, week four is a little different, for you will be allowing the visions to occur of their own volition, as it were. This means simply going with the natural flow of your imagination as opposed to the direction and control you have exerted during the previous week. The benefit here is that the element of spontaneity is given its due measure (another prime facet of visualisation ritual) and that eventually you will acquire the ability to synthesise both the willed and instinctive elements of the imagination. That is, the direction of the action you wish to make happen, with creative images that just seem to 'occur' of their own free will. (There is more on this directive/receptive aspect in week five.)

Setting The Scene 1

Imagine yourself descending a sheer drop that appears to go on forever. On and on you fall, faster and faster with no apparent end in sight — only blackness — as the ground you expect to reach seems to recede further and further away. In the minute distance you see a tiny pinprick of light speeding towards you, getting larger and larger, until you realise you have tumbled into a brightly lit cave. Your fall decelerates rapidly and you fall ever so lightly, as if a feather, upon the cave floor. You pick yourself up in this dazzling, subterranean enclosure, apparently alone, and then a kindly voice announces from behind, 'I'm so glad you could come, I've been waiting for you.'

125

What happens next?

Who is the owner of this friendly, reassuring voice?

Setting The Scene 2

You are in an old, barren house ascending a flight of stairs; timber creaks with every footstep and your shadow plays sinister games on the wall as you continue to move upwards. The staircase is lit only by a bland moonlight, a wash of cold, pale blue, and you grip the handrail tighter as you climb ever onwards towards the mystery which beckons. Finally it is there before you, that great oak door, magnificently carved and boasting a fine, though oversized brass handle. Just what lies beyond the door is for this instant still a mystery, yet you slowly turn the handle and push apprehensively against the oak. The door starts to yield.

What, or whom, do you find on the other side?

What then happens as a result?

WEEK FIVE: 'ROLL CAMERAS'

After last week's foray into the often uncharted regions of one's imagination, we are back to a specific exercise which serves as an attempt to blend the directed and free flowing elements of the imagination. One ought to discover later, by a natural process, that having created various specific images and brought them under the control of the will, spontaneous elements arise and 'fall into place', adding a kind of autonomous effect as the visualisation comes to life of its own accord. Though the ritual must be backed by the control of the will, and by necessity under its direction, such spontaneous living reality as referred to above must be the ultimate aim of the visualisation.

After having ensured a relaxed mind and body, create in your mind's eye a picture of some favourite person of yours, perhaps a well known actor/actress, 'pop' star, sportsperson, TV personality, politician. Work upon this image until it is fully detailed, for instance, the clothes they happen to be wearing, where the person happens to be situated, and the general aura that is presented. Approach the person as if you were well known to them, shake their hand and — without further ado — begin a conversation with them. The location and topic of conversation (to name but two) are items which you yourself will create and direct within your imagination. However, you may find that your visualised celebrity begins to assume a 'real' and lifelike quality, where it is no longer necessary to put the words into their mouth, so to speak. If you will persist with this scenario for long enough, the effect will resemble that of objective creation, where the person you have selected acts quite independently and without any prompting.

Having reached this stage in your visualising, feel free to experiment with other 'favourite people': visit their home (what kind of place, is it?), take a long walk through the countryside with them (what do you see on your travels, what do you both talk about?), go to a restaurant with them, etc., etc. Needless to say, one can have great fun with this exercise, but the fundamental value lies not in its enjoyment, but in participating in inner plane work that actually looks and feels (for want of a better term) 'real'.

Self-Analysis

Did you find, after several exercises, that the imaginary elements in your mind were just as — if not more than — real as the physical persons and objects they represent?
Did you find, during your conversations, that your chosen subject would begin to talk and converse about things which you yourself would not normally consider?

WEEK SIX: YOUR GOAL

Here is probably the week you have been waiting for the most! At this stage, the image making faculties of your mind will be ripe and ready to make constructive use of, so why not turn them into a beneficial working tool? Surely, everyone aspires to some kind of goal or objective: the large, luxurious home, a dream holiday for two, enough money to enable one never to have to work again. Or perhaps your ambitions are somewhat more humble? Perhaps at this stage they ought to be, at least until you can claim some degree of success in your visualising on the outer level, that is, having employed 'mind power' successfully in attaining some desired goal. Let us thus commence moderately, turning our attention to some goal which can be realised within a matter of a few months, though which is not so insignificant that one would regard it barely worth waiting for.

Perhaps one would select some material luxury item; whatever the object of the ritual, *make sure you really want it!* This advice, on the face of it, sounds slightly ludicrous, for surely one knows when one really wants something. Unfortunately, this is not always the case, for many of us lack the ability to focus our energies upon one specific desire and persevere until we have it, simply because something replaces it in our affections and we decide we really want *that* instead. Yes, it's the proverbial case of the child looking at the toys in a shop window, hence the above advice.

When you are entirely sure of your desire for this object, and are prepared to spend several weeks visualising for it, then *write it down* on a sheet of paper; write nothing else than the name of this object and keep the paper handy. Additionally, you might try cutting out a picture of this object, perhaps from a newspaper or magazine, and pasting the picture immediately beneath what you have just written. The next step, of course, is to create its likeness within your — by now fertile — imagination and settle down to visualising, providing of course that you have prepared for your session in the required manner, i.e. with relaxation.

The next stage consists of acquainting yourself as fully as possible with your desire; capture in your mind a picture that is vividly alive, dynamic and ultimately real — as real as the intended object itself. For instance, let us suppose that you are visualising for a video cassette recorder; you would — by necessity — use associated images that pertain directly to that object, and here is where another Golden Rule makes its entrance: visualise yourself already in possession of your goal, not about to possess it. This means, within the context of the example, that you would not imagine yourself in a situation whereby you are *going* to acquire a particular object, but where you already have it. This particular Golden Rule, I must stress, is fundamental to *all* kinds of visualisation.

One may then proceed to create within the mind's eye, scenarios relating to the envisioned goal, where one is presently enjoying the benefits of the desired object. Does this goal in your imagination make you feel uplifted, wonderful, happy? It should do. (More on this in the following section.)

Self-Analysis

Were you able to decide upon the object of desire almost immediately, without too much thinking about it?

Do you sense a kind of uplifting feeling when your specific goal is 'seen' in your imagination?

Points To Remember

The object you are visualising for ought to be attainable within a relatively short space of time in order that you may credit yourself with a minor 'success', and thus be encouraged to progress eventually to 'major' objectives.

The images you are working with must be clear, detailed,

vivid and strong, in short, (here goes that word again) real.

The visualisation must portray yourself as being already in possession of the desired object.

WEEKS SEVEN AND EIGHT: HAVING FAITH

With reference to the line in the previous section about feeling 'uplifted, wonderful, happy', these two weeks are dedicated to intensifying the ritual with the all important element of *emotion*. I asked that seemingly glib question since invoking positive feelings about the object of one's desire is an absolute necessity in visualisation, yet, as so often is the case, the simple *idea* of the goal is sufficient to lift one's emotions to a feeling of positive expectancy. Thus, either you are quite naturally excited about this desired object during the ritual (in which case the likelihood is that you will attain it much quicker), or you will be required to 'stir up' certain emotions synthetically, in order to impress the unconscious with your ideas. (The affirmation exercises in the next section may prove helpful in this respect.)

The kind or quality of feeling to which I refer is one of faithfulness, a belief in one's goal coming true, which is possibly the one most important aspect in the practice of visualisation. For the following two weeks, persist if you will in the attempt to get through to the unconscious, impressing it in such a way that the idea becomes real to the inner mind. One particularly useful technique towards this is the 'As If' method, which is operated at times other than when you are actively visualising, and, dare I say, complements your rituals tremendously. As I have pointed out, during your imaging ritual you must see yourself already having achieved your goal, and it is this spirit of having 'already got' that we now intend to transport to the outer life. That is, for instance, the times when one awakes, catches the bus to work, goes to lunch, returns home, etc.; it is during these moments, when one's attention is focused upon the environment, that we can subliminally influence the unconscious mind. So much depends on the particular goal, so in order to use 'As If', or what Charles Haanel calls 'reversing the evidence of the senses', one must adapt in a creative way. For instance, to take our rather trite example of the VCR, one might go out to purchase a blank video cassette, enlist in a video library (and carry the membership card around in a handy pocket), or purchase the latest video film magazines.

The example, I admit, may sound trivial, but the technique underlying it has method in the madness, and it will work if carried out in the correct spirit. By this I mean with a complete suspension of logic, a disregard for the facts as one sees them, and a refusal to doubt or disbelieve. The facts are those related to the present situation — the fact that one has not yet achieved the goal — which, to the rational part of the brain is glaringly obvious. However, the 'As If' technique can, and will, succeed in colouring such stark, black and white reality, encouraging a spirit of expectancy and faith in the future. Whatever method one employs for 'As If', one must ignore the rational mind for a while and be prepared to falsely believe, as it were, that one's desired goal is a definite reality.

Self-Analysis

At the end of this two-week exercise, do you find it a little easier to believe that your goal will manifest?

Points To Remember

Getting through to the unconscious depends upon removing the obstacle of logic, the evidence of the senses at present, if we are to convince the inner mind of the certainty of our desire.

Remember, the accent is not upon what *is*, here and now, in the concrete world, but upon what is going to be, or more correctly, what has (mentally, at least) *already* happened.

WEEK NINE: AFFIRMATIONS

By this time, it is to be hoped, your faith is beginning to increase and your visualisations are now clearer and more powerful — no less than five sessions per week, remember. What follows is another exercise in intensifying your magical experiment, that of autosuggestion, a method geared towards the all important impression upon your unconscious. Credit is due here to one Emile Coué, whose famous autosuggestive line, 'In every day, and in every way, I am getting better and better', must have worked wonders for the patients who earnestly made use of it. Coupled with visualisation, such a technique can only enhance and stimulate the inner mind to a point whereby all fear, doubt, disbelief and lack of confidence disappear beyond the horizon. The method is simple, effective and *clever*. Its ultimate aim is to induce a certain kind of belief within the unconscious so that the object to which it refers is duly attracted in the outside world. Repetition is the key, and so long as one is fully relaxed, the unconscious will start to believe your affirmation — whether it is true or not.

During this week, you will perform two kinds of affirmation, namely written and verbal. Take that sheet of paper with the name of your goal upon it, and simply write above, 'I have now successfully attracted to me, my   .' Keep this sheet of paper with your affirmation (proudly boasting your new found success) somewhere handy, somewhere where you will quite often casually notice it. If you have succeeded in acquiring a picture of your desired goal from somewhere, then so much the better. Also, one might like to intensify this subliminal affirmation process perhaps by making photocopies of your written statement, and placing the copies in such places where your attention will be repeatedly drawn to them. For instance, try sellotaping one to the bathroom mirror, upon the bedroom wall; use one as a bookmark in your current favourite read, or leave one lying face upwards in an oft used drawer.

The second type of autosuggestive method is based not upon visual effects (i.e. the automatic response to certain words and pictures) but upon those of the aural variety. This means that you are going to listen attentively to yourself making various affirmative statements, reacting wholesale to the emotive power of the words thus used, again to get through to the unconscious. As you complete each visualisation during this week, you will apply the finishing touches with one or more of the following self-affirming pronouncements. (One must bear in mind, as a matter of course, the need to be fully relaxed and to approach the exercise in all *seriousness*.) Simply repeat your chosen affirmation slowly, over and over again:

1 'I draw upon the forces of the Universe and now attract to me the goal I desire so intensely, and so shall it be.'

2 'I give thanks to the Universe for bringing me my   ,knowing that this represents only one small fragment of my inner potential.'

3 'I am happy to receive my   , knowing that its arrival results from my union with the inner forces.'

4 'I am filled with a sense of wonderment at the magical results I have just achieved, and shall from now on create many more realities like this.'

Self-Analysis

Are you able to experience some abstract inner force, some power, virtually 'agreeing' and cooperating with you as you speak out loud your affirmations?

Points To Remember

Affirmations are but one technique for impressing the reality of your goal on to the unconscious, and effective results will soon occur when this communication is made.

This impression is made possible (despite however silly the techniques may appear) since the unconscious does not perceive rationally and logically, and will work with whatever material it accepts, whether true or not.

WEEK TEN:
MEN AND WOMEN OF WISDOM

Although on the face of it this exercise may appear a little unorthodox, it is nothing less than another experience in mental assimilation, though in this case the affirmations come from the words of various prominent thinkers. By virtue of this, it is to be hoped that such sayings will lend an element of faith to one's visualising, simply because to hear meaningful aphorisms of the wise minds of our time which confirm one's inner desires and imaginings, is positively encouraging. No more, or no less, than that.

1 'Ask, and it shall be given you; seek, and ye shall find, knock, and it shall be opened unto to you.' (Matthew 7:7, 8)

2 'When any object or purpose is clearly held in thought, its precipitation, in tangible and visible form, is merely a question of time.'   (Lilian Whiting)

3 'Believe me . . . imagination creates the reality. This is a great cosmic law.'   (Richard Wagner)

4 'Every moment of your life is infinitely creative . . . Just put forth a clear enough request and everything your heart desires must come to you.'   (Shakti Gawain)

5 'Seeing's believing, but feeling's the truth.'
                      (Thomas Fuller)

To begin with, select an aphorism which is particularly meaningful to you. Continue with your specific goal-imagery during this week, impressing certain evocative images upon your mind's eye. However, whilst doing this, simultaneously recite aloud, and slowly, the aphorism you have selected, thus bringing image and affirmation together. The emotive power of your chosen quotation will combine with the power of your imagination and impress that faculty within the unconscious which attracts things to you. (My favourite affirmation is that of Wagner's.) Perform this technique over and over, slowly, at least ten times, and of course, repeat it each day/evening of the week.

Self-Analysis

Do you find that your selected quotation 'confirms' the goal image in your mind, by invoking a feeling of certainty and faith?

Points To Remember

Believe me . . . Imagination creates the reality!
Happy visualising.

BIBLIOGRAPHY

Andersen, U.S., *Three Magic Words*, Wilshire Book Co., 1954

Brennan, J.H., *Getting What You Want*, Thorsons

Brennan, J.H., *Experimental Magic*, Aquarian Press, 1972

Capra, Fritjof, *The Tao of Physics*, Fontana, 1983

Chetwynd, Tom, *A Dictionary for Dreamers*, Granada, 1972

Chetwynd, Tom, *A Dictionary of Symbols*, Paladin, 1982

Conway, David, *Magic — An Occult Primer*, Jonathan Cape, 1972

Crowley, Aleister, *Magick* (Edited by John Symonds & Kenneth Grant), Routledge & Kegan Paul, 1973

Davies, Paul, *The Forces of Nature*, Cambridge University Press, 1979

Davies, Paul, *God & The New Physics*, J.M. Dent & Sons, 1983

Dee, Nerys, *Your Dreams and What They Mean*, Aquarian Press, 1984

Emerson, Ralph, *Essays, (Vol. II of Complete Works)*, George Routledge, 1900

Fitzhenry, R.I. (Ed), *The David & Charles Book of Quotations*, David & Charles Publishers, 1986

Gawain, Shakti, *Creative Visualization*, Bantam, 1982

Haanel, Charles F., *The Master Key*, Psychology Publishing Co.

Jung, Carl G., *Synchronicity — An Acausal Connecting Principle*, Routledge & Kegan Paul, 1972

Koran, Al, *Bring Out The Magic In Your Mind*, A. Thomas & Co., 1964

Mulford, Prentice, *Thought Forces*, Bell & Hyman, 1979

Ophiel, *The Art & Practice of Getting Material Things Through Creative Visualisation*, Samuel Weiser, 1967

Peale, Norman Vincent, *Treasury of Joy And Enthusiasm*, Unwin Paperbacks, 1984.

Ramacharaka, *Fourteen Lessons in Yogi Philosophy*, Yogi Publication Society

Russell, Bertrand, *A History of Western Philosophy*, Unwin Paperbacks, 1978

Samuels, M & N, *Seeing With The Mind's Eye*, Ramdom House, 1976

Sartre, Jean Paul, *The Psychology of Imagination*, Methuen & Co., 1972

Swami Rama & Swami Ajaya, *Creative Use of Emotion*, Himalayan Institute of Yoga Science & Philosophy, 1976

Watts, Alan, *The Wisdom of Insecurity*, Rider, 1974

INDEX

141

If you have enjoyed reading this book, other titles in the Quantum list will be of interest. These include:

The Dream Lover, Transforming relationships through dreams,
by Les Peto

Dowsing for Health, The applications and methods for holistic healing
by Arthur Bailey

Life Cycles, The astrology of inner space and its application to the rhythms of life
by Bill Anderton

Psychic Sense, Training and developing psychic sensitivity
by Mary Swainson and Louisa Bennett

The Survival Papers, Applied Jungian psychology
by Daryl Sharp

Astrology's Complete Book of Self-Defence
by Robert Parry

Seeds of Magick, An exposé of modern occult practices
by Catherine Summers and Julian Vayne

The Healing Hand Book, Discover and develop your healing power
by Patrick Butler

Ask your bookseller for full details on the complete range of Quantum titles.